when
it
rains

Also by Maggie MacKellar

Core of My Heart, My Country

Strangers in a Foreign Land

MAGGIE MACKELLAR

when it rains

VINTAGE BOOKS
Australia

A Vintage book
Published by Random House Australia Pty Ltd
Level 3, 100 Pacific Highway, North Sydney NSW 2060
www.randomhouse.com.au

First published by Vintage in 2010

Addresses for companies within the Random House Group can be found at
www.randomhouse.com.au/offices

Extracts from Simone de Beauvoir's *A Very Easy Death* © Simone de Beauvoir,
1969, 1997. Reproduced by kind permission of Editions Gallimard, Paris and
the Estate of Simone de Beauvoir c/o Rosica Colin Ltd, London.

National Library of Australia
Cataloguing-in-Publication Entry

MacKellar, Maggie, 1973–

When it rains: a memoir.

ISBN 9781741669602 (pbk.)

MacKellar, Maggie, 1973–
College teachers – Australia – Biography.
Widows – Australia – Biography.
Loss (Psychology).
Bereavement.
Adjustment (Psychology).
Life-change events – Australia.

378.120994092

Typeset in 12/17 Sabon by Midland Typesetters, Australia
Printed in Australia by Griffin Press, an accredited ISO AS/NZS 14001:2004
Environmental Management System printer

10 9 8 7

The paper this book is printed on is certified against the
Forest Stewardship Council® Standards. Griffin Press holds
FSC chain of custody certification SGS-COC-005088. FSC
promotes environmentally responsible, socially beneficial
and economically viable management of the world's forests

FSC
www.fsc.org
MIX
Paper from
responsible sources
FSC® C009448

Return

Return often and take me,
beloved sensation, return and take me –
when the memory of the body awakens,
and an old desire runs again through the blood;
when the lips and the skin remember,
and the hands feel as if they touch again.

Return often and take me at night,
When the lips and the skin remember . . .

Constantine P. Cavafy (1912)

For A. and C.

1

I'M STANDING AT THE END OF LANE FOUR at the Cudal memorial pool. It's just after lunch on club championship day and the kids are about to swim their butterfly races. The pool pulses with the sounds of summer, and in the distance the trees and rocks on the town common shimmer in the heat. I'm timekeeping. I have been all morning. I'm surprisingly good at it.

Over the antiquated PA system, participants for the Fathers' Race are called. This is not a revelation, I've known about it since Thursday. I'm prepared for it – I've warned the kids that it's happening and offered to swim in it. They laughed: a mother in the Fathers' Race! In front of me, four kids line up for the fifty-metre butterfly. The starter says, 'Take your marks,' he presses the button and the kids hurl themselves up the pool. I watch as they turn at the twenty-five-metre mark and, arms madly circling, head back for a close finish. I glance at my stopwatch out of interest – it looks like a fast race – but I haven't pressed the button. I'm sure I pressed the button, yet the screen is blank.

It's four years since he died. I knew there was going to be a race for fathers today. I'd carefully schooled my heart against his beating absence. Yet in an instant I'm stripped and the present is sucked away. I've come to see that sorrow moves in endless circularity, yet always manages to shock in the most ordinary moments. Standing by the pool and looking at the blank screen of the stopwatch, I feel again the lurch and pull of that place where past and present collide. The hard ground radiates heat and I cannot escape the chasms in the earth. I slip in between as the rushing horror swallows me once more.

Just over two years ago, I packed the kids in the car, put my furniture in storage, took a leave of absence from Sydney University, left my house on the Northern Beaches of the city and returned to the farm in Central Western New South Wales where I'd grown up. It felt like the riskiest thing in the world to turn my back on a secure wage, and yet the only possible solution to the difficult juggle of single motherhood and a career. I told myself I was coming for just a moment, a break, a few months in the country to allow me to catch my breath. It would be a short pause in my career, a time with my kids when we didn't have to worry about schedules, child care, late nights marking essays or writing lectures. I could put a bit of the country into them, give them a love of open spaces, imbue them with an independence that the cloistered city life steals from childhood. It would be a time when I would regain control of my emotions, catch up on some sleep, impose some sort of discipline on my increasingly out-of-control two-year-old son and ground my ethereal seven-year-old daughter in something solid and real.

I wrote to my uncle and aunt to ask if they would have us to stay for three months in the cottage at the bottom of the garden. By way of reply, they drove their ute 350 kilometres over the mountains to collect everything that wouldn't fit in the back of my car. Standing on the side of the road, we surveyed the scattered belongings spread along the footpath. Bikes, boxes of books, pot plants, some kitchen essentials, a baby's cot, a high chair, a fridge and a rocking horse all piled into a tottering load for the trip. Kids rode bikes up and down the street. A young, handsome couple pushed their new baby in a pram worth more than my uncle's ute to the park at the end of the street. Teenagers walked between my possessions on their way down the hill, surfboards under their arms. This was a nice street in a nice suburb filled with nice people. Lapping at my feet was the debris of my life. Yet, when I look back now, all I can hear is the poet Anne Carson's warning: 'Sometimes a journey makes itself essential.'

I couldn't tell you the exact moment I knew I had to go home to the farm, but once the thought embedded itself, it was like a grass seed. At first I ignored it, then it was in so deep the irritation was all-consuming. Quite simply, after coping for so long, I couldn't cope for another day. I had to leave that city street, pack my small family into the car, travel over the mountains and hope for some redemption on the other side.

∽

My body, suddenly, carries two stories of loss. I'm heavy with them, made cumbersome and slow. One is easy for people to recognise. My mother died of cancer. I watched her age twenty-five years in eight weeks. In the night, when she was already a long way away, I would climb onto her bed, curl my body round hers and shake with the intensity of my desire for her not to go.

I want my mother and I rage that she was taken from me. Yet, amid this devastation, there was companionship. People know what to say when your mother dies. They instinctively feel your loss, recognise their own fear in the marks on your face, the tremor in your voice, the dark lake of your eye. People know about cancer – they know it kills, they know someone it has killed. They fear it may kill them. People know and in their knowing you are not so alone.

My other story marks me as different. It is more silent and more savage, it is not pure and no one knows how to approach it. Not even me. This I also carry in my body, but it's hidden deep below the surface. It is a subterranean river. It haunts my dreams with a hollow, hoary roar. In the daylight I hear its echo in the emptiness of my laughter.

Somewhere I lost my husband. He slipped away from me in a whirl of fear and confusion. I tried to hold on, but he was too heavy and the water was too strong.

There are so many ways to tell his story. Each has its own particular truth. Each is difficult to contain, slippery in meaning, in time. After he died, I sought clarity by writing in strict chronological order the events that led to his death. I took each day, sketched its beginning and end, recalled each mood, read into every silence some sort of message. I wanted to trace the trajectory of his breakdown, to look for clues about spaces into which I could have stepped and saved him. I wanted his past to speak to me. As I wrote, what emerged was not clarity, nor understanding, nor peace; what was left was a chaotic scrawl filled with pain – and, looking back, an inevitable end.

So which strand of truth deserves to be told first?

My closest companion of eleven years, father of my five-year-old daughter and an unborn son, died with intent. He was in hospital, in a supposed 'safe' ward, a place he couldn't voluntarily leave. He was in a session with a doctor and his parents; he walked out of this session, scaled a twelve-foot wall, ran to a cliff and placed himself in an impossible position from which to be saved. In the end, despite the efforts of rescue workers, he fell to his death.

This was not a new thing; this was something he had attempted before in the preceding few months. And yet this was such a new thing that I, his wife of more than a decade, still cannot quite accept it was my husband at the centre of an inevitable drama played out upon a cliff top in the wind and rain of a squally July afternoon.

2

WHEN I CAME BACK TO THIS COUNTRY, I lay down. Dust covered me, grasses dipped seeded heads and whispered their secrets, ants marched their pattern across my skin. My wounds give off their own light. I glint and shimmer, pinned upon the ground. Pressed between earth and sky, I think, be careful, don't say *home*, don't say *safe*, don't *say* anything.

Fragments rise up. Words in straggling sentences trail their half meanings through the air. I find myself straining to hear, to capture a trace, a sense of where the words would take me if I allowed myself to follow.

When we were young, my husband and I spent three months kayaking and climbing in the Alaskan wilderness. We then spent another three months living in a tiny shack outside a small town. Lucerne flats, no electricity, no running water, no car, no phone, no one knowing where we were – somewhere in Alaska, somewhere in the year 1996. I was twenty-three years old, unexpectedly pregnant, unemployed and happy. He was chopping wood, carting water, cooking dinner, running the ten-mile round trip into town for milk, happy. We'd walk in the evenings, through lucerne that waved at our waists, and talk of the future, of study, of life with a small child.

Our time in the mountains was a shape-altering experience. We lived in fear of falling off the edge, of drowning in icy seas, of being swept away by swollen rivers, and over the three months I gradually got to know my body – its boundaries, its needs and, perhaps most challengingly, its insignificance. I stood on top of a forest on a windswept tundra and watched as a mountain of rock simply fell away. There was no warning, no wind, no clap of thunder, just one moment a mountain, the next not. I was humbled and appalled. The land, the ground I stood on, warned me and I didn't listen.

When we came back 'inside', that is we returned to a place of settlement – buildings, shops, homes – I realised that I understood my body differently. I now knew I could command it to go beyond what I'd thought possible – to paddle harder, walk further, climb higher – all in extreme weather conditions. My body was stripped of surplus, it wasn't carrying anything more than it needed to survive and when I asked it to make a leap, to place a hand or foot in a particular place, it just did it. Before this I'd enjoyed my body, had fun with sport, with love, but I'd never taken it seriously like I took my mind; I'd taken it for granted.

The unplanned pregnancy scared me at first. Climbing with the beginnings of a new life within me made me acutely aware of my femaleness, my vulnerability, but mysteriously it also strengthened my determination. After Alaska I looked on my body with a little bit of awe. When we returned, I stood on the earth differently, I felt connected to subtle changes in wind direction, in temperature, in light. I reacted to the space around me almost without thinking. My body had become a powerful thing.

Now, after these two deaths and a birth, I once again occupy a foreign place, but I can't feel anything through my body.

I roll over in bed and the movement is ponderous. I know how my breasts fitted perfectly in his hand; now they are some shape I don't recognise.

∽

We arrived in winter to a house that creaked with cold. I hibernated and the space was close around me. For the first time since he got sick, I felt safe. The smells and sounds of the land were comfortingly familiar. At night I fell asleep to the sound of sheep moving outside my window, and I woke to the stillness of the frost. There were no sirens, no humming of traffic, no passing footsteps, no murmuring of voices, no pressure to be anywhere. Just the rhythm of nature, the pleasure of lying adrift under a full moon, or wrapped in the blackness of a moonless night. This peace brought sleep, but sleep brings dreams.

My new home is a small rectangular cottage built by my grandparents. It's a little building, which they added to as their family grew, adjacent to the main house; across the garden but separate. It's a building outside its time: my grandmother insisted on floor-to-ceiling glass. The drama of the seasons shifts through this room; unfortunately this also means it's freezing in winter and boiling in summer.

The kids settle happily. Outside their windows the garden is sparse in winter quiet, beckoning them to explore its deeper secrets. We have three weeks of school holidays before Lottie will start at the local public school. I have taken the semester off teaching and only have marking, then I'm free till the end of summer.

It's a good time to have arrived as my uncle is lambing. The farm runs a stud of White Suffolk sheep and the ewes are brought into the paddocks close to the sheds to lamb. Here they become ladies-in-waiting. Early every morning and again on dusk, my uncle makes his rounds, sorting out the newly lambed ewes from the about-to-lamb ewes, and the twins from the triplets and singles. Slowly he works his way through the mess. Ewes who have only a single lamb, or ewes who are experienced mothers with twins, he sends into the nursery paddock, where they will stay a couple of days before being moved across the road. First-time mothers, or mothers who are having trouble looking after twins or triplets, are placed in little paddocks dotted around the lambing shed. These pod paddocks have water, shelter and plenty of feed as they are only used at lambing time.

The new mothers shepherd their lambs into the protective cover of the trees. Then there are those who are struggling – perhaps a twin has died, or there has been a difficult birth and the ewe is exhausted, or perhaps there are three very tiny lambs to look after and an inexperienced ewe with not much milk. All manner of problems can occur – an infection in the lamb or mastitis in the ewe. This group ends up in the lambing shed, which is filled with pens bedded down with straw. It's a lovely place: a long centre aisle with pens down either side, a pile of hay in the corner, and protected from the wind and sleet. Lottie helps to prepare pens for expectant mothers and makes nests for the newborn lambs. The whole set-up reminds me of a busy maternity ward, with my uncle acting as chief obstetrician, midwife, ward sister and hospital administrator rolled into one.

In this way the school holidays pass in a blur of little jobs. There is none of the desperation I have felt in the past of finding activities to fill the days. Already the kids are too busy to worry about school; too absorbed to be sad; too tired with running all day, playing outside, feeling useful to have trouble going to sleep. They are high on the freedom of the space out here, and don't seem to miss our little house on the Northern Beaches, nor their friends.

One July day, Lottie grows cold sitting on the fence and watching the road as it curves around the hill. A ute appears, pulling a float. A pony gets off the float and looks about with wide eyes at his new home. My daughter wraps her arms around him and breathes in his solid warmth. I remember my mother standing watching the same moment on the same patch of dirt.

This pony is big for a small person and he's not pretty, but he's reliable and quiet and, even better, he's tall enough for me to ride. His ragged chestnut coat is brushed to a shine over the next weeks, and I come to love his big head, with its little pony ears and extravagant blaze of white down his nose, looking out of the stable window, waiting for us in the morning to let him into the paddock. At first he's cautious with his affection – can he trust us, is he going to stay here for good, do we know how to look after him? I watch him working out how much he can get away with. I watch him on those first few rides – he is careful to keep Lottie in the saddle. Every time she loses her balance, he stops moving until she is safe again.

3

WHEN I FIRST LEARNT MY MOTHER HAD CANCER my husband was already dead. My mother and I stood in the doctor's office and swallowed air as if it were already our last breath. We faced each other and no words passed between us. In that moment I was exposed and the space around me emptied. We groped for each other and held on. My child, her grandchild, drove a truck around the waiting room. We hung above him and looked down at him from a great height.

Laid out below was the landscape of our lives. A soft wind drifted up from the valley floor and bore us upwards. I felt my arms begin to stretch and my feet scrabble for purchase. I felt life surge through me and I watched as the life poured out of her and the wind carried her away.

Now, only months after her death, I've returned to her childhood home. She left here as a young woman to move to Sydney, where she met my father, who was also a country boy. It's the place of my childhood memories, for we spent our school holidays here. I see my mother in every shadow. She is all around me but, and this is the trick of death, she is nowhere. I can't even see all of her anymore. Shapes loom up and distort her face, her voice. Yet, I wonder, is it her or me who has been erased?

At the clothes line under my feet she has engraved her name in the concrete. I hang the clothes and her hands appear before me doing the same job in the same place, with baby clothes that will be bleached in the sun and frost. I lean into space towards her, but instead of more of her, I see my older brother. His presence is relentless. He moves into the frame, blocking her. I can still see her hands and yet instead of her voice I hear his silence.

My older brother has no ordinary voice. I can recall my mother carefully outlining his capacities and his limitations, which marked out the boundary of her world. He went to a special school; he doesn't talk; he makes funny noises and is sometimes embarrassing to be around; he can be destructively manipulative. He is obsessive. He also has a deep and wicked sense of humour; he is opinionated and smart; he is compassionate and incredibly gentle if he likes you. Though he has no voice, he has words and he uses them as weapons. He speaks through a computer, into which he types, painfully, one letter at a time. These words are heavy, as if the miracle of their emergence gives them a weight disproportionate to their meaning.

Some of the first words he wrote, after two decades of silence, described my mother's hands hovering close to his face. His words stole her, as his actions have always done. He said he saw butterflies shimmering over his eyes. Her hands drew the world for him, possibilities only she was brave enough to see. Her hands sheltered and protected and were scarred by him.

After my parents' divorce, my father moved to Melbourne and my mother looked after every part of my brother's life. Then, terribly suddenly, it was my younger brother and I who had to face the practicalities of caring for him. He was living with our mother in Sydney when she got ill. We tried not to panic. Her treatment was immediate and brutal; she was instantly incapacitated, shunted into the parallel universe of the sick. The community drew around us. My aunt, who looks just like our mother, travelled from country Victoria to help with her nephew. She's practical, she needed no looking after and her presence eased our burden. The day she arrived, an old friend staggered at the door, thinking she was our mother miraculously healed and returned from hospital.

৵৵

Those first few weeks after our mother's diagnosis, we were riding a bucking bull and being thrown from side to side by the bad news and what we thought of as good news, but which was actually just less bad. Every so often we'd manage to sit on the bull's back, and we'd feel the muscles beneath and the power dormant and quiet. But it would only be a moment, just enough to jag at hope again.

In the midst of this wild ride I picked up a hospital brochure with information for patients and their families on my mother's diagnosis. Cancer with an unknown primary site meant they could only guess at treatment. Unlike breast cancer or lung cancer or any of the other cancers that are labelled and known, cancer caused by an unknown radical cell is difficult to treat and almost impossible to survive, because the direction of its growth cannot be predicted. I was astounded by the statistics and watched myself refusing to believe the printed words. They couldn't be talking about my mother. The pamphlets didn't mention survival. They used euphemisms to soften the facts which, when read without padding, said simply: months probably, a year if you're lucky. But the thought that my mother was going to be killed by this cancer had not penetrated to a place where I could understand the words. I put the pamphlet down.

෨

My mother had been diagnosed for three weeks. She had nine more weeks to live. I worried about getting my research grant application in on time.

෨

I too marked my mother's hands. Perhaps not so deeply as my brother. But when my husband died and my baby was born, she supported me so I could go to work. She said nothing, or, more accurately, not much to signal that she thought I was exhausting myself at my expense and hers, not to mention the needs of my children. Yet part of my drive came from having watched her surrender herself for our family, for my brother. I was desperate not to be her.

There were countless times when she had the children overnight so I could work. She'd drop by in the afternoon and scoop them up while I returned to my desk. She would often have all three – my two small children and my older brother. I'd arrive in the evening and find her exhausted, in the midst of happy chaos. The kids were bathed and fed, their souls filled with her love. They had been reading books, writing poems, painting, sewing, cooking, but I could see the rising waters of her exhaustion. I pushed my conscience down with gifts of appreciation, packed the small people into the car and left her to face the burden of my brother alone.

It was my mother's hands that received my baby boy as he slipped from my body. She held him and sang to him, her hands firm around him, swaddled him, patted him, learnt him. I hadn't wanted her at the birth, thinking it more important she look after Lottie. But she came anyway and told me later that she had to be there, even if it was to sit outside.

It was a relief to let her hold him. To watch her loving him. I followed her lead. This baby, whom I'd sheltered and who'd grown stronger within me even as his father's mind was splintering; this baby, who was my constant companion through trauma and despair, had finally arrived. I didn't fall for him as instantly as I did for Lottie. It was strange to meet this person whose insistence on being was, at times, so urgent it pushed aside the most violent emotions. In the end, it was my mother who taught me to love him. She held him high, she held him to her. Her delight was contagious and my desire to love him fell as suddenly as the water that heralded his arrival. His little body and its urgent needs shielded my head and heart.

I'm conscious of portraying my mother as something of a saint. But she saved me after my husband died. She showed me how to go on with life; how to balance the sadness with an enjoyment in the simple ordinary moments – the miracle of my baby's first real smile, a small child's delight at learning to ride a bike. She infused me with her practicality. When Lottie couldn't go to sleep at night, terrified that if she closed her eyes I would be swallowed by the same darkness that stole her father, my mother cautioned against overreacting. She listened patiently to this little girl's distress. She didn't distract Lottie or shut her down, nor did she react as I did, in frustration. She insisted that what Lottie was going through – the anxiety, the nightmares – was perfectly normal and should be allowed to run its course. She refused to buckle to the temptation of imagining some long-term pathological explanation for Lottie's compulsive behaviour. And she was right. The bedtime rituals slowly dissolved the terror. Time worked quietly and chipped away at her fear.

In those early days after my husband died, when Charlie was still a tiny baby, my mother would take Lottie up to a park near her house to ride her bike. Surrounded on three sides by bush, the park looks straight out between the North and South Heads, and the water below is always filled with boat traffic. Ferries steam back and forth, and huge cargo ships with rusty sides shepherd slowly through yachts and leisure boats.

My mother considered exercise a key to sanity and sleeping well. She told me I could not expect Lottie to sleep well if she was not physically tired. So, while I fed the baby, sat with him and learnt to love him, she spent an hour or more running around behind Lottie as she learnt to ride her bike without training wheels. My mother found the bike on someone's council clean-up pile and wheeled it home, then took it to the local bike shop for new tyres and some streamers to sling off the handlebars. The streamers are the only thing Lottie notices – not the black paint job, scratched and rusty after years of service and more years of sitting in someone's garage. It didn't take long for it to become something of a ritual to load the bike in the back of the car and take Lottie to the park, to ride and ride. They would return exhausted, their cheeks touched by salt air and something of the expansive view of the harbour park where the wind scours the grass.

My mother's hands were sixty-four years old, weathered, beautiful. They were soft and hard and they held no duplicity of emotion. They didn't love and hate. They were not tender and violent. They never offered me the world and handed me hell. They were constant: I miss them purely.

4

I FEEL HIS HANDS ON MY BODY. Still. They draw me out. Catch me when I hadn't intended to respond; tease me, seduce me, collapse me. But then I remember his hands close up, the pattern of the hair on the back of his fingers, and my desire is swamped with dread. For all I can recall then are his fingernails bitten away, the cracks that appeared on the sides of his fingers and his hands shaking with agitation.

On the farm, I no longer have the distraction of work to hide from what happened to my husband. Instead I turn to the physical to find a release from the images in my head. I drag myself across the ramp and head off down the track. I've left Charlie asleep and Lottie drawing horses; my aunt is working in the garden. It is a huge release to have the freedom to leave, to shut the door behind me for an hour and know the kids are happy; they haven't been dumped somewhere. I haven't had to buy time for myself. I don't have to get in the car, I can just walk out of the door and go. I slog my way down the track to the lucerne flat. Too fat to run far, I walk and run alternately until I'm too puffed to run at all. The air is moist and a low mist hangs over the trees near the creek. It's been raining, and above the trees insects have swarmed. I wipe the sweat from my eyes. The insects hover and the trees look as if their spirits have taken a physical form. A family of kingfishers swoop and glide, their azure breasts cut through insect clouds.

At our first meeting, I grasped his hand and felt the calluses beneath the skin. Hard, strong and healthy, hands marked by gold flecks that caught the light. We paddled together on Pittwater. He was at home on the sea and I was thankful I could balance on a surf ski and follow him across the water. I was seventeen, he was twenty-six. We landed on a narrow beach and set off up the steep cliff. We climbed the cliff and his hands pulled me up and showed me a new world.

I polish those moments, the back story of our life together. I shine them and place them tenderly on the mantelpiece for all to see. Out of these frames my husband's death is even harder to understand. The man on the mantelpiece loves his job as a lecturer in Outdoor Education, he's an enthusiastic and creative father, he's fit, delicious to look at and a wonderful lover and caring husband. Yet, even as I polish the memory of our marriage, his hands rise up and destroy all the moments we shared. Instead of the warmth of these moments, all I see is him yanking a handful of hair from his head, from his eyebrow, from under his arm. His hands became the tools he used to wound himself. Burns from the heater were an easier pain than the one in his mind.

∞

After my run, I make for the wood heap. It's still cold. I seek movement, repetition, cold air against my skin, the handle of the axe in my hand, the heaviness of wood straining my wrists as I choose a block to chop. I don't stop until my shoulders ache, until my wrists reverberate with the shock of hard wood against steel. When my breath is ragged and my face hot, I look up and see the rim of my world. It's quiet and it's lonely.

Lift the axe and let it fall. Over and over it bites into the stump. In my first weeks I couldn't see the place I needed to strike and instead made a pattern of dents on the heart of the tree. Small chips flew into the air and the stump gave back nothing I could burn. My aunt, several decades older than me, seized the axe, smiled, and showed me how to follow the growth of the tree; showed me the age rings and how to hit the trunk just so. Underneath her blow the stump fell in a concertina of perfect-sized burning blocks. All through winter I banged away at those old stumps. I'd load the wheelbarrow and push it around the back of the house and along the veranda to the wood box. I discover muscles of memory hidden beneath my skin.

∾

We'd got him into a private clinic and I slept for the first time in weeks. The first morning after his first night there, I brought him a small photograph in a wooden frame. From the picture our daughter looked straight out into the world – confident, beautiful, loved. I left the room for a moment, reassured by his stillness. I'd worried all through the night, and I was

23

relieved to find him still whole. He seemed reasonably relaxed and while he finished his breakfast I walked quickly to the bathroom. Something, some sense I'd learnt not to ignore, turned me back. He had taken the picture out of its frame and was using the glass to cut the skin on his wrists. Bile rose in my throat – it was so pathetic, so futile. I pushed back the door and he went berserk. Those hands that had loved and soothed me, and held our daughter, grabbed and smashed and hurt. I called for help, but I knew the only person to calm him would be me. He was like an animal, bereft of reason. He fought and struck and I weaved and dodged, hoping if I pressed him and soothed him with the pattern of our love, he'd remember and be calmed.

I had him. He was quiet beneath my touch. But then came the staff with their pills and needles, and their medical knowledge. I watched as they sedated him and the drugs shifted him still further away. The drugs made him worse, he grew more confused and more agitated. They gave him drug after drug, each one heavy with hope, but he had disappeared and I was faced with a raging beast who was no longer any person I recognised.

He'd hurl a chair, break a picture, throw a bowl of fruit. We were in a police car. In Emergency of a major hospital. In a locked and windowless room. In another hospital. All the time my love fought and fought – it would not surrender. Over the chaos of doctors and nurses and locked doors and safe rooms and wards, it would not die even as it was rejected, even as it was assaulted with half truths and outright deceit, even as I retched and retched, sick with the knowledge that this illness was destroying my imagined past and future.

I watched the nurses laugh as I arrived laden with home-cooked food, nourishing teas. He was too sick, but I set us a little table and insisted we try to share a meal. He bit the food as if it could kill him to swallow. I took out the pile of essays that I had to mark and settled in for the evening. He paced the room, the corridor, the edge of the high wall, and his agitation growled like a wolf between us. The young nurses seemed to smirk as I left in the late evening. They thought they'd seen it all before, and perhaps they had, but I was determined we wouldn't be like everyone else.

Now I look back and see only an arrogance that insisted we would be different; that resources, contacts, *reason* would somehow save us. I carried my pregnant, awkward body past the goldfish bowl of their station and waited for them to release the lock on the door. I was getting in their way, I knew. But I didn't care.

All the books I read, all the people I spoke to, cautioned against throwing my love before this illness. Yet what else could I do, how else could I be? My insides curled themselves away from me. Swallow it, I told myself, and stand.

∞

I look for different ways to keep busy. It's years since I've been on a horse, but I saddle the new pony and the familiarity of his swinging stride shifts something in my head. As we follow the line of the creek, my husband's grip loosens and I'm fighting back.

The poplars are bare and the pony shuffles his way down through layers of leaves. Wild ducks startled by our noise beat their way up the creek. The pony shies. We haven't had much winter rain yet and the creek bed is dry except for a few deep holes. I'm hunting for rams who've hidden themselves in the quieter corners of the creek. Most of their mates are making jostling progress across the flats and eventually up to the sheep yards. The pony is telling me there's something around the corner. We push our way through, over half-rotten logs and past murky water; the pony climbs the banks to avoid getting his toes wet and I give him a hearty whack to remind him we're on a mission. Ahead of us even I can sense movement.

We round the bend and are greeted by four big rams annoyed that their mid-morning snooze has been disturbed. They charge off and in a sudden plunge we are through the stagnant pool and after them. I'd forgotten how quickly a horse can go from standstill to a dead run. We fly up the steep bank and it's only old instincts that keep me in the saddle. I can't help but laugh out loud at the sense of satisfaction the pony has with himself as he heads the rams into the main mob and drops back to a walk to tail them to the yards. He flicks his ear at me as if to say I am lucky that one of us knows what we're doing.

The dogs work the back of the mob, criss-crossing their tracks, singling out stragglers to snap at, throwing a quick glance at my uncle to make sure all's well. I trail quietly up the paddock on the pony. Charlie hangs out of the window of the slowly moving ute singing as the sheep string out around him.

5

I simply want to be dead.
....
no grove [   ] no dance
no sound

If Not, Winter: Fragments of Sappho, 94

OF THE JUMBLE OF POSSESSIONS that stood on the footpath outside my house in Sydney, none felt more important than the boxes of books solidly sitting among the high chair and cot. When my uncle arrived with his ute to help me pack up, he shook his head at these boxes. I could see him suppressing a question as to why I needed so many books. Me, I wanted the room to sway with them.

Since I've stopped teaching all I've done is read. It's ironic. We're meant to read as part of academic life – we get paid to read – but I could never find the time. Instead of reading I'd be rushing to pick up the children from child care, tennis, after-school care, dance, swimming, and madness – instead of reading I'd mark essays. Instead of writing history I wrote lectures on subjects I knew nothing about, such as the Harvester Judgement (believe me, it's important) or, worse, Federation. I wrote for grant applications on subjects I knew I'd never find the time to research. I fantasised (and I wasn't alone in this) about spending the money I was given for research assistance to pay for child care, just so I could get into the archives to read.

If I did read, it would be in a mad scramble at 5 am to try to keep up with the students I was teaching. I passed colleagues in the corridor who threw comments over their shoulders about the latest book they'd finished. I sat in on seminars fighting the overwhelming desire to sleep while others around me were engaged and eager to contribute from the latest research publications they'd read. I had the sensation of being broken down on the side of a freeway.

The publication of a first book in any academic career should be a big moment. It's the culmination of years of work and the amount of thought, reading and archival research that's gone into it will never be repeated once you hop on the teaching treadmill. A first book normally comes out of a PhD thesis, and mine was no exception. Shortly after my husband died and Charlie was born, my thesis was accepted for publication and I was lucky enough to be selected to work with an experienced editor to turn the manuscript into a book. We did the work, the book was published and launched, and in the middle of this my mother was dying.

The book was about women's responses to place on the frontiers of Australia and Canada. Those who survived there had one thing in common: an ability to find a reflection of themselves in the new land they had settled. None of the women were necessarily defined as intellectuals, though many wrote memoirs or poetry, or painted, but they all made an enriching link between the places they lived in and their success and survival as mothers, wives and individuals.

My mother came to the book launch. She sat in the audience with a turban round her chemo-bald head. Her granddaughter sat on her knee. The night was bittersweet and any sense of achievement was swallowed by the battle laid out so clearly before her.

Though I had another research project mapped out, which would explore a new generation of women who were forging connections with land, after my mother died the research held no life. I couldn't concentrate on it; my intellectual curiosity – something that had always driven my reading – was replaced by apathy. What I needed was a blank page, and what I craved was dirt under my fingernails.

After I made the decision to take a break from the university, I carefully chose the reading material I would take with me. Instead of the latest in post-colonial theory, I packed pyramids of words written by those whom I hoped would be fellow travellers. I read outside my comfort zone, turning to the ancients to see if they had any greater sense of surety. Occasionally I tripped over a sentence and would be forced to lie on the floor. 'I know one thing: all is grief for you.' The scene is the dramatic climax to Euripides' *Herakles*, written at the end of the Peloponnesian War, when

Athens was defeated by its overblown ambitions. I had come across it in a recent translation by Anne Carson. Amphitryon is speaking to his son Herakles. Herakles has just slain his wife and children in a fit of insanity. The scene is bloody and desolate and Amphitryon's words seem to cut through the madness of Herakles' actions as he defines his son not by the murders he has committed, but by the grief he will forever carry.

In her essay introducing the plays, Carson asks why tragedy is so vital an art form. For her, the tragedy becomes a frame that can be put around our grief. Inside the safety of that frame the violent expression of grief and rage can be played out without 'you or your kin having to die'. Nobody, writes Carson, wants to 'go down into the pits of yourself all alone'. Instead, we are drawn to stories in which actors sacrifice themselves and dive into our collective darkness.

Her words strike a chord, but then a quiver runs through me and I'm forced to ask what happens when the players inside that created frame are not actors; what happens when it is you caught between grief and rage, when it is you who must go down to the deepest pit to search for the way to ascend to the light once more. What does Euripides and his like say for you then?

Walking in the evening through the heavy scent of grass broken by the heat of the day, the willy wagtail sings his lament and the sound carries across the garden and down over the flat. I find I can ask these questions of myself from the safety of this solitude. Though I find comfort in Euripides' plays, though they signal all I'm grappling with is not unique, they do not show me the path back to myself. The longer I remain trapped in Carson's frame, the closer I come to erasing myself and, like Herakles, becoming defined by grief itself.

For me it is the act of writing that unlocks the frame. I pin my tragedy onto the paper and with the precision of an anatomist take a scalpel to separate memory from bone. Perhaps if I can peel the layers of skin from its torso, it will stop having the power of a dark shape in the night. By writing, I risk sacrificing my deepest intimacies, but by writing, I control the shape they become.

∾

I'm washing my mother in the shower. She's so weak. She gropes for the wall and shakes with the effort it takes to stand and let the water stream over her. It's soon after her diagnosis and we haven't yet gathered the paraphernalia of the seriously ill to help us through these daily tasks. In fact, her illness is so fast that by the time they arrive – the shower chair, commode, walking frame, the all-white utility anonymously attesting to our entrance into the world of the very sick – my mother is too ill to be at home.

But that day. That day I walked into her bedroom and searched for her. She looked tiny, unrecognisable from the woman I had left only three days before. Then, she was happily settling into her new townhouse, alive to the possibilities of the future. We'd sat in the courtyard and talked of the garden she would put in. We ate Thai food and drank wine. She talked about the colour of the kitchen cupboards, the splashback she would choose for behind the sink. She talked as if there were going to be a tomorrow. The next time I saw her, I watched her as she slept and I knew she was going to die. She seemed to age even as I helped her to the shower and washed her back.

I didn't want to. I didn't want to love her in this way. I wasn't ready to help her as she died. The warm water sluiced over her skin and washed me too. I was shaken by the exchange between our bodies. In the cold feel of my mother's flesh I met myself, as if death already stood beside us both.

I write these words and feel small, incredibly selfish, unable to be the person I'd always imagined myself capable of being. That moment in my mother's bathroom defied the march of seconds and minutes and hours and days and years. Do you see that I met myself and was afraid? I was afraid my daughter would one day meet herself in me, and that there was no point in living, for time had already ordained my end. I stood and washed and wept, for her and for me and for she who follows.

How do we learn to accept that we are all flesh and blood and must die? How do we grow wise enough to realise that nature doesn't distinguish between the deserving and the undeserving? How do we grow brave to face our own death?

It's an ingrained habit to reach for words when I circle these unanswerable questions. I write as the memories rise up and then I must ask myself, why commit them to paper? Do I write to seek the trace of life; to find the entrance, the moment it became something else? I seek words as I seek reality – in small bursts. Perhaps if I can shape the past, capture it for a moment, it will take a form I recognise.

After my mother died, a good friend sent me book after book. They piled up beside my bed and toppled quietly in corners of the house. I reached for them in the early morning when the baby woke. I read by the radio, coffee in hand, as the light of day pressed against the windows and the traffic began its roar. It was the desire for connection, for a common place, that made me read Simone de Beauvoir's account of her mother's death in the 1960s. She wrote about her mother's body and I found a thinker who echoed my own terrible unease at ministering to a body that felt as if it were mine.

> The sight of my mother's nakedness had jarred me. No body existed less for [me]: none existed more. As a child I had loved it dearly; as an adolescent it had filled me with an uneasy repulsion: all this was perfectly in the ordinary course of things and it seemed reasonable to me that her body should retain its dual nature, that it should be both repugnant and holy – a taboo. But for all that, I was astonished at the violence of my distress.

Like de Beauvoir, it's this violence I come back to when I think of these moments – physical distress wrestled with my mind, which insisted I stay and minister to my mother. At war with my will, my body would resort to guerrilla tactics – my stomach would heave and I'd have to rush to the bathroom.

I go over these events in the lengthening light of early spring. Our days have developed something of a routine. In the morning I walk with the kids down the track to meet the school bus where it stops at the ramp. In the city our trip to school was filled with fluster and tension, traffic jams and mothers and nannies dropping off their precious charges at the school gate. Sometimes the tension got so high that the local police supervised drop-off time.

Now our mornings might be flustered as we run late, but it's a different pace when all you're racing for is the bus that'll wait for a flying figure on a bike pedalling furiously down the hill.

On Lottie's first day, we walk into the classroom and meet her teacher. Surely this woman was ordained to be my child's teacher. She greets us with a frank gaze. I see her mentally roll up her sleeves and say to herself, 'Here is a child I can help.' She is a countrywoman, she has strong family values, she is a mother, she is a lover of nature and she comes forward to welcome my child.

There is something wonderful about a small school. When we arrive, I'm struck by the straightforward simplicity of the kids. They play together before school in a great helter, a complicated game of tip, backwards and forwards across the grass playground. As soon as Lottie is spotted standing rather forlornly next to me, a gaggle of small girls split from the main group. They swoop and gather Lottie into them. Suddenly it's me standing alone and unsure at the gate as she sprints across the grass in the midst of the laughing group. The next morning she assures me she will catch the bus. And that's it – she's in, established.

Most mornings Charlie and I watch the bus disappear round the bend of the road and then walk slowly home. After morning tea we might go out into the paddocks to help my uncle with the sheep. Then, with any luck, a sleep for Charlie and reading and writing for me. The day has a sleepy peace to it, bookmarked by the school bus. In the afternoon, we walk to the stables and saddle the pony and while Charlie rides his bike, or pretends to drive the tractor, or hammers nails into bits of old wood, Lottie rides her pony round and round the yard until she is eventually confident enough to progress to the chook paddock, then the lambing paddock, then the cow paddock and finally into the great wide world beyond.

The creeping, quiet days signal something else. Longer days mean spring is on its way, summer galloping on its heels. It's then I must face the reality of returning to the city, to my job, to picking up the pieces of my life. I pace through the day, agitation skulking in the shadows behind me. The house is full of blowflies. There's a small patch of gauze loose on the door, but surely all of them can't have entered through this hole. They seem to have hatched out of the warm air itself. They buzz at the front of my mind. They signal the end of winter, the rushing of time, the threat of decay. I hate them. But with the relentlessness of a tide, I'm picked up and carried forwards into the warming days.

6

WHILE I WAS STILL LIVING IN THE CITY, I dreamt I walked along a dirt track. Above me the sky was lit with stars. On either side of the track I could feel the country pressing. The land was heavy with presence, in my dream it breathed – rising and falling in a gentle cadence – marking each step. I walked for a long time following the track. There was low scrub on either side and though I could hear the tiny heartbeats of scuffling animals, and once the loud guttural grunt of a pig and the reverberation of its heavy body through the bush, I was not afraid. The country started to open out and I left the gravel of the track and walked out onto a vast claypan. In the distance, the ghosts of trees hovered and swayed, drawing an edge to this space, while beneath the bowl of sky my moonlit shadow cast an eerie shape. I wasn't wearing shoes, the clay came up between my toes and the red earth felt silken. It was lonely, but it didn't feel empty. As my eyes became used to the moonlight and to the length of the space, I saw, or I think

I saw, the white glint of bones shining in the ground. For the first time I felt uncomfortable, as if I shouldn't be there, as if the land were not humming for me but for the dead it already held.

I woke shaking. Getting out of bed, I ground my feet to the floor and padded along the bare wooden boards of our tiny semi in this very suburban beachside suburb. There was no silken touch of mud, just the midnight drone of the city and on the other side of the thick wall a mother and her middle-aged daughter. These women never moved around in the night. Did they hear me? They must hear my baby. Surely he is the loudest baby ever born. Each night I brace myself for his screams. His rage at being in his bed seems almost transcendental. He hurls himself against the side of the cot, opens his mouth and cannons of sound ricochet off the walls.

In the bright light of morning I slink along the fence, up the front steps and into the car. I carry bags – a day-care bag, school bag, library bag, handbag and my laptop, whose hard edges bang against my leg. I wave to the woman next door, mustering cheeriness from somewhere. She looks on with pity, concern, irritation all over her face – who could tell. Charlie is strapped into the car seat and contained at last. I lean against the car, take a breath and coax Lottie into the car with murmured encouragement about how much better school will be today than yesterday, trying to think of a way to help her overcome her nerves at navigating the fraught social terrain of lunchtime play. I suggest going to library, though I know this is inadequate. I drop Lottie off and square my shoulders at the solid snarl of traffic. Charlie sleeps for first time since 4.30 am. At the traffic lights, I try to remember what my 10 am lecture is about, scanning the reading list for my two-hour honours seminar after the lecture. I remind myself that I wrote the course – I should know what's in the readings. I drop Charlie at child care. Then I prise his octopus fingers from around my heart and shut my ears to his screams.

∾

Despite the fact I was not coping with juggling my job, my kids and my loss, I fought against the obviousness of my need to escape. For if I left, I was relinquishing a hard-won position at the university. Instead of ambition, I was now swamped with a longing for silence, for a place where I wasn't forced outside myself, a place where I didn't anticipate a random knock on the door, where I didn't have to gather my courage in case I met someone who'd see the brilliant light emanating from my wounds. More than this, my body was collapsing, no longer the strong thing I once could rely on. It betrayed me. Tears leaked from my eyes at the most unexpected moments. A hacking cough carried me through dreams of my mother's last days. My throat itched and burnt. At night I couldn't sleep and by day I couldn't stay awake. Friends knew I wouldn't ring, instead they phoned to warn of their arrival, they entered the house and made it alive with laughter and noise, food and wine. I hurried to get the kids to bed so we could sit on the deck talking, drinking. But all the time I wanted a place where I could stop trying, where I didn't have to be quite so brave.

One of the problems I faced in the city was the difficulty of disciplining my increasingly headstrong two-year-old son. Everything was a fight, and because there was always a bigger agenda going on – I had to get to work, I had to write a lecture, I had to mark essays – those fights were being won by the smallest person in the house. I was caving in on everything, from what he ate, to what he watched on TV, to what time he went to bed, to when he had a shower. And it was unfair on Lottie; the two of us were being dominated by this powerful toddler. But by moving away from our small house, where I was always aware of the neighbours, I dramatically shifted the power play between Charlie and me.

So today when Charlie decided he wouldn't walk any further and started his usual throw-down, red-faced screaming act, I walked off and left him to it. The effect of this on him was electric. He upped the intensity, but I kept walking until I reached the garden fence. I went inside and made myself a cup of tea and took a book to the front gate to sit where I could see him and he could, if he chose to open his eyes, see me. The determination of the child was impressive. He flayed himself on the earth for nearly an hour before lifting his head, climbing wearily to his feet and following the track up the last 500 metres to the garden. I greeted him at the door with a hug and a 'glad you've made it home'. We sat down and had morning tea with my aunt; no one commented on his red eyes or his hoarse voice.

After morning tea he played until happily climbing into bed and falling asleep before I'd even checked on him. On mornings like this I dare to feel that in this space we have a fighting chance of making it.

The dream in the burial ground seemed to hint at a resurrection born out of the earth, but the place where the earth lay silken on my skin was at the end of a very long journey. Sitting here in the sun, in a moment of reprieve from my small son's demands, I question whether I can ever walk far enough to find that place. But, at least for the moment, I'm no longer braced against seeing my husband. The shock of not having to block him out of the front of my mind is almost enough to make me fall over. I've learned not to look for him. I've shielded my eyes from seeing. But now in this new place, where I don't expect him to knock at my window, where I don't expect to see him running down the street, perhaps I can allow myself to start that walk.

7

How do I tell you about us? About him and me, I mean. How do I stitch a pattern where you might peek at what I had and what I lost? I'm being seduced in my dreams, he's pursuing me, he won't leave me alone and my anger is being unpicked, even as I hug it closer.

You think you know someone. You are so sure of someone. Then, one morning there is this new thing. This new thing that is a very old thing. A thing that has been buried so deeply that the skeleton, when it appears, is prehistoric. It is something you don't recognise as being of the world that exists between the two of you – you and the person you thought you knew. It is a dinosaur. It is a monster. You feel as though it eats you alive.

One day he says, 'This has happened before.'

'What has happened before?'

'Losing my mind,' he says.

'Oh, really? What do you mean?' I'm scrabbling, for air, for the ground, for something to hang on to.

He says, 'You don't know everything about me. There's something I've never told you.'

'Oh.'

Then there appears a terrible pit. Knowledge is a strange and powerful weapon. Our life together, the last ten years, is sliced up.

'What do you mean, you had a breakdown?'

'I spent six months in and out of hospital when I was eighteen.'

'I spent my nineteenth birthday in the psychiatric ward.'

'They wouldn't let me out.'

'I actually don't remember how long I was there – sometimes it feels like it was my home, sometimes I forget I was ever there.'

'They diagnosed me.'

'They never diagnosed me.'

'I walked out and never suffered from such a moment again.'

'Until we met I suffered from these episodes but never told anyone.'

The contradictions darken the sun.

I have been loved, cherished, celebrated and I have been deceived, manipulated and treated as less than nothing – all by the same person. In the broad light of day, I can see no track back to my husband. It's only in the dark, in the stillness of night, that he appears before me. He comes softly; he comes to me from a cave. I retreat and still his body presses. I've withdrawn, laid my weapons down, turned my back and still he pursues me.

The dreams have returned, though it's long after he's gone. When he first appeared to me after his death, my anger was so fierce it broke through the crust of time and I hurled abuse at him to stay away. I woke sobbing, my eyes as dry as ice – but the next night and the next night and the night after that, he returned. I greeted him cautiously. I found myself questioning the certainty of my anger. Could I really be so angry? Could my heart really be so heavy? Could our future be so destroyed?

Now, I'm being seduced.

He coaxes me out. Dares to touch me. He may be back in my dreams, but I force myself from sleep to remind him that he is no longer in my life. How could he think my trust would tremble and reform before his touch?

But my dream body and his dream body deceive me. They know each other so well. Soon, though it's a long time since he died, he's back in my bed. He visits me with increasing frequency, but I resist. There can be no happy ending here. Say, I forgive him. Let him stay. Say I do that. Where does that get me? Does it get me to peace? I think not. It leads to a place where I'm naked under the sky, where the world around is edged with mountains and the earth underneath is scoured by fierce cold, and heat and wind.

And yet desire creeps up on me and I crave his touch. If I hold my rage as a shield he will never find me, but then I lose again, for I cannot remember, ever, the taste of him. His absence is so heavy. It makes me move ponderously. He lit me. Sent me high, beyond space, beyond time, he defined the edges of me. Every time I go near this place, my bitter rage pulls me up short of allowing him to love me once again. How dare he leave me? How dare he lie to me? I'm so angry, I really wonder how he dared.

Do other people mourn with anger and rage? Grief books say it's a 'stage', but they never tell you your body burns with it, or how the anger scars. I hear people say they rub themselves with violence. They seek love affair after love affair. They become an empty vessel into which they pour sex, drugs and drink. They search outside themselves for someone, something to reach them. I wish I had that solution, but even if I had the freedom to do any of that, even if waking with a hangover, waking with a stranger were possible, I don't do them. I wouldn't get him out of my head that easily.

Some nights I've attempted to muffle the memories with wine. Yet there are only so many mornings you can wake to a headache and a two-year-old child. It just doesn't work. There's no one else to get up, to make porridge, poach eggs, warm milk, dress small people, give the day the shape that satisfies the demands of a toddler. Even the fact that I can't lose myself in drink makes me angry with him. There is no one left to pick up the pieces, no one left to rescue me from this mess.

So I go back. I force myself to shed him. I force myself to stand in the open under the sky and peel him, layer by layer, off my body. I'm screaming as I do this. Can you hear me? It hurts so much to leave him behind. To turn and face a future without him, I have to strip him from me. He's the barrier between me and a future. He's a buffer between me and every person I meet. He distorts my voice. He distorts my vision, and I can't see around him to the person talking to me on the other side. They say something and I realise they don't know. They can't see there's a body between them and me. If I'm to survive and not be consumed by him, I must place him piece by painful piece on the ground.

∞

After his wife died, C. S. Lewis wrote: 'I look up at the night sky. Is anything more certain than that in all those vast times and spaces, if I were allowed to search them, I should nowhere find her face, her voice, her touch? She died. She is dead. Is the word so difficult to learn?'

Is death so difficult to learn? I push his body from me and think, why, yes, my friend, indeed it is.

8

IF I COULD TAKE OFF MY GRIEF, if I could peel it back from the places I carry it, would it stand up by itself? My grief for my husband seems so random. The triggers are not obvious. It's twisted in my body.

I remember his back as a tapestry of muscle. Sitting in front of him in a kayak as we paddled the Prince William Sound in Alaska, I would force my body into the rhythm he had established. I couldn't see the muscles across his shoulders, running down his ribs, meeting across his stomach, but I could feel them pushing the boat through the water. I can feel them now, his body and mine paddling across the big water. I was not afraid when I was out with him. The shifts in the wind, the movements of the tide, the subtle adjustments he made to accommodate the swell all signalled his easy knowledge of the sea. It wasn't an environment in which I felt at home. I was always searching for the land, measuring my strength against our distance from the shore. Could I swim that far? Forests of kelp drifted below my paddle.

Later, we lay on top of a cliff and looked out over the sea to snow-capped mountains. The midnight sun sat lightly on the horizon before it rose again on a new day. I was cracked by his salt-encrusted smile, by the movement of his muscles propelling me over water. And now I'm cracked again and the memories drown me.

After my husband died, I was assaulted with images. The disorder of them undid me when I was working. Work was mostly an escape. I needed the discipline of having to front up and be professional, face an auditorium of students who had no idea of the chaos of my home life and, what's more, didn't care. It was a relief not to have to account for my mental state, not to be observed for signs of strain. So it was shocking in those moments when my husband intruded into this world. I would stop in the middle of a lecture as he appeared, golden like a cat, supple and polished, before the bars of my cage.

Away from the lecture theatre, away from the bars that keep these memories at bay, I struggle with questions, trying to wrestle them into something meaningful. They perch like a crow on a barbed wire fence, ready to pick out my eyes. Their threat is a lingering presence – no matter how often I chase them away, these questions circle back and size up my strength.

I try telling myself the most comforting version of his death. The one where he felt he had no choices left; the one where he saw for a moment the terrible damage he had done, and felt weak before his inability to be a husband, a father, a provider. This impulse has a kernel of courage at its centre. I like this version, it's the one I conjure up when strangers press me for details of how my husband died. It's neat and sort of fits those fairytales we're brought up on, in which the handsome prince dies to protect his true love. I tell myself he could have thought for a moment his death was the easiest way to protect me from him. I'm not wholly convinced by this argument.

There are other versions, which are not so comforting or sanitised. There is the one where my anger at his deception and inability to stay in treatment spits in derision at his choice to run. In this version, I see him as a coward, as someone who would flee rather than confront his past. In this version I despise him.

But I'm honest enough to admit that there is another story that plays itself out in my head. This one travels along the tracks of my own inadequacies. It's the one in which I blame myself. Why didn't I see him struggling? Why didn't I understand the depth of his despair? What was wrong with me that he wouldn't stay in hospital and that he didn't, ultimately, see our lives as continuing together?

I don't want anyone to answer these questions for me. I'm rational enough to understand how depression changed him. And I'm able to argue myself through the reasons behind my inability to save him. But still the accusing voice echoes across the distance, and it's not until I lay out all the arguments side by side that my reason is shored up and he diminishes, slinking away from the tracer fire of my defence.

I walk into the paddocks, stride up the steepest hill I can find, and sometimes the physical exertion is enough to break the crust of anger in my head. The anger holds everything in, it sits like salt around a dried-up dam, defining the retreat of moisture, of life.

Every memory I have of us is compromised by what has come since. Yet the memories persist, or is it he who persists? I walk harder and my muscles burn as the sweat runs down my back. Was he struggling even when we were in Alaska? Was I just blind, was he thinking of escape way back then? These questions stream into the blue of the sky and are swallowed by the silence of the land around me. I've come out here to put myself back together, but he stalks me through the days. Each scene we lived I re-enact. I keep walking and slowly the anger, the betrayal, the constant questions dissolve somewhere between the black of the storm clouds, the lit green of new growth on a eucalyptus tree and the screech of a pink galah.

But at night he returns, and I'm helpless to run from him. I climb into bed, drift into sleep and then his body shudders and I feel it in mine. The memory of his movement is steeped in my blood. It's as if I can't look at him in my daydreams, but when I dream in the dark, he appears so close that I question again the reality of his absence. My arms make the shape of him, my body shifts for him to squeeze in beside me, and every morning I wake and think for a moment, he's just getting me a cup of tea. In fact, he never is. So I stay in bed, buried beneath the blankets, unwilling to face another day. A song rises in my head, 'Heavy blankets, heavy blankets cover lonely girls', and I wonder again, how did I get to be here?

He did this to me just after he died and it went on for six months, until, in the January of Charlie's babyhood, after a spring of being up at night and sleeping in snatches through the day, I was woken by a thud as a stone hit the bottom of my soul.

During those months, I'd wake and ascend the layers of my mind till I reached the present and could acknowledge he was dead. Each night I'd freefall, meeting him on every cliff, seeing him at every window, hearing him behind each closed door. He had been gone so many times in the crisis of his illness, I'd grown to expect him to be gone when I woke and then to turn up in the most unlikely places. I'd grown to trust his absence wasn't permanent. Even when he was locked in hospital, he would arrive at my window in the middle of the night; at a birthday party; behind a closed door, where I would find him curled, shaking, under the desk. How many safe wards did he escape from?

So every morning I'd crawl back from the place where he was still alive, gathering the parts of me that refused to believe he was gone, forcing my scattered senses back to a whole knowledge.

But that January morning he tumbled through my mind and could fall no more; he finally hit the bottom of me, and when I opened my eyes I knew he would not return. Each layer of me knew. And I closed over that knowledge and got up to feed the baby.

So I don't understand why he is back in my dreams, nearly three years later. And now he's haunting me. I see him running. My heart jolts as he disappears around a corner ahead of me. I never see his face, just the glimpse of his heels. I see his back moving away from me. It gives me a fright. Maybe he hasn't really gone. I never saw his body. They wouldn't let me.

9

THROUGH MY WINDOW the paddocks are a brilliant green. It's our first spring here. When we moved, the country was cold and bare and desperate. People were hand feeding or selling valuable breeding stock, pushing sheep and cattle onto the roads in an attempt to save enough of them to rebuild when the dry broke. And now, suddenly, unbelievably, it's over. This is the biggest spring in thirty years.

Out of nowhere my publisher calls and asks if I can come to Melbourne to talk about a new project. I push down hope at the possibility of not having to return to Sydney for work and get on a plane. It's the first time I've left the kids since my mother died. The sensation of being without them is like adrenalin dripped into my vein. The shops of Melbourne beckon, but I don't fit into anything I pick off the rack. The body in my head and the reality of my post-baby figure don't match up. I buy shoes instead, fabulous shoes that, despite my broadening figure, make me feel alive.

Winter is banished when I return. Blossom is wild on every tree, the grass has turned from a fluorescent tinge to riotous heights, and all seemingly overnight. The creeks are flowing and the place looks as if it carries no stock as the cattle and sheep disappear into a wall of feed.

When Lottie trots through the paddocks, all I can see is her hard white helmet rising and falling above the grass, her pony grabbing mouthfuls of rich feed as he goes. The poor pony spends his days and nights locked in a bare yard with a scrap of hay to sustain him, while on the other side of the fence the grass grows tantalising and abundant. It's the fate of all ponies in a big spring to spend their lives in a yard, waiting for the feed to dry off. So he makes the most of his outings and trots through high feed, his small charge on his back, and, despite his grass rein (which stops him plunging his head to the ground to eat), he still manages mouthful after juicy mouthful, till his neck and chest are stained green from the foam.

The days are a procession of sunshine and rain. The earth is warm and, despite my resistance, I'm being coaxed out of myself. From the breakfast table I can see where the sheep have been grazing – the paddocks behind them are neat and shorn. They look as if someone has moved over them with a lawnmower, paying particular attention to the edges. It's a view that transforms the drudgery of making breakfast for two small children into an event to linger over. I sit at the table and stare at the view while Lottie reads aloud her home reader and Charlie plays with his Weet-Bix. Time is slower, less painful; perhaps, I think, I will learn to live again.

My uncle grazes his stock on a cell system. The big

paddocks are divided into smaller cells by light electric fences and grazed and manured intensely for a few days, then the stock move to the next paddock. It's reminiscent of older grazing patterns, of nomadic herders who camp for a couple of days in one spot until the feed is gone, then move on. The intensive grazing seems to entice the native grasses back, it feeds the soil with all the manure and the advantage for my uncle is knowing exactly how much feed he has in front of him for the season. For the kids and me, it means lots of work mustering sheep every few days. But really we don't need to help, the stock have quietened down so much through the constant moving that all my uncle needs to do is stand at the gate and send a dog around them. We help anyway, trotting round the back of the mob, pretending to be useful.

One old blind ewe has been left behind the main mob. She's by herself and I watch as she works her way around the paddock. She uses the fence line to find water and seems to manage her days in a logical way. I wonder if she will survive. She has the nervousness of the outsider. To rejoin her with the rest of the mob would mean bringing the whole lot up to her. If I run past her and she senses me, she takes off in crazy flight. Better to let her be.

∞

Very quickly my mother faced blindness, even before the cancer struck visibly. It seemed unfair that she would lose her sight just as she was able to gain some independence from my older brother, who was in the process of moving into his own accommodation. I watch the ewe circle the paddock and realise I've forgotten how adaptive she had become. Every day we made small adjustments so as not to startle her with the extent of her blindness. Not that she didn't know. But we wanted to save her from the pain of what she couldn't see.

But after the lump on her neck grew, we didn't talk about her eyes.

In late November, my brother took her to the doctor. By then, a small army of friends had formed a roster to clean the house, look after my other brother, drive my mother to chemo, take over the running of her life. I crept around the edges of all this. I knew she was going to die. I don't know how I knew. I didn't know what to do about this knowing. I didn't know how to face it. I had nothing of that icy calm with which I faced the other crisis. Then, one day, it was on me.

When we were children, we spent our summers on the Central Coast. Our house was perched on a cliff. It faced south to the wind; east to the sun. In the evening, at the end of a hot day, we watched the southerly beat its way up the coast. The wind pushed the water far beyond the protection of the cliffs, ruffling the glassy surface into small mounds. From the deck we watched the mounds peak and trough, waiting to see the white caps form as the wind pushed deeper into the water, then waiting again for it to hit us. There was always a point before it really arrived when I thought the front would go round us. Always that moment of surprise – the lull while my mind caught up with the rush of wind on land.

'It's just the chemo,' the nurses said. But it wasn't. It was sitting on the veranda watching the storm swoop up the coast and imagining for a moment that it would miss us.

Two years after my husband died, my mother was so weak she couldn't get up from the bed. Though she had been continually and violently sick for days, I knew it was not weakness that caused her toe to drag, to catch behind her ankle. Something terrible had swooped. It was sitting on our shoulders. It was closing its wings around her, shrinking her so she could be swallowed.

Who knew that dying was such hard work? I've watched animals die. They get a look. They disappear into themselves and after a while you can't reach them. The dying is easier than the living. They retreat, find solitude, and in moments their head is twisted back on itself and life is gone. If it gets too hard, we help them. A bullet, a sharp knife to the throat, an overdose.

The nurses murmured outside the door as I gulped air, 'Brain cancer, it's a good way to go. It's worse on you than her – she doesn't know anymore.' Bullshit. Don't tell me this, don't pat down my distress. There was nothing, nothing, easy about how she was dying.

When we were told by the doctors our mother was dying, we had to search through a jungle to hear their meaning. We had to take a machete to their words to find some sort of clarity. Our mother was going to die, but they still wanted to treat her. Our mother was going to die, but they wanted to cut a hole in her head and deliver the chemotherapy straight to her brain. Our mother was going to die, but before we could stop them they had tapped into her spine and delivered a dose of chemo. Were we missing something? Had someone among the ever-changing team of doctors offered hope where there had been none before? Only under aggressive questioning did they acknowledge the treatment offered no hope, only more time – possibly.

My sorrow has arms and legs, fingers and toes. It has a mind and a heart: it bleeds and dies. It breathes and sobs, howls and laughs. It is full and it is empty. It is resilient and it is weak. I walk around in it. It is anger and rage. It has a memory but no name. It is ancient and outside time. It whimpers in the night like a small child. It is terrible and unapproachable. It is vulnerable and needs to be held. It is impenetrable, an armour that cannot be pierced.

∾

C. S. Lewis wrote that grief feels like fear. He was right. I rise every day and swallow the terror. Every night I creep to the safety of my bed and breathe once more. The kids are safe, we've all survived the day. I lie there and go over its events. I tell them again and they become memories. Carefully I add them to two piles – one that makes my mouth dry with dread and one that whispers of redemption. So I see the sickening moment of a pair of flashing chestnut heels and a little girl flung to the ground. That belongs in dry-mouthed dread. It's joined by the memory of the stinging instinctive slap I gave my small son for hitting me in the face. There's the feeling of inertia that sits heavy on me in the evenings and early mornings. Is it fear or is it grief, or just depression, that prevents me from moving? I can't go on living hidden away as if my only need is ensuring the children are happy and healthy, clean and well-fed.

Then there's the other pile, in which a little boy is hanging out of the ute window singing as the sheep stream over a new paddock. Or climbing the gravel pile with his big shovel, ready for an afternoon of construction work. The evening light as it settles on the rocks and the trees and the hill; the swinging stride of a pony that seems all eagerness to please, and the look of delight on Lottie's face as she jumps a log long thought of as too high. Standing in the vegetable garden with the sun pushing in and out of the clouds, I plant lettuces for summer, beetroot and snowpeas, covering them with mulching hay, wondering if we'll be here for the harvest. The air seems thick with birds and, as I plant, it pushes away thoughts of the future.

Grief paralyses. It muffles and distorts and, yes, it feels like fear. In fact, where does one start and the other end? I met them together and they are as difficult to separate as muscle from bone.

Was it fear that caused me to retch even as I looked at my mother? I sat beside her and reached out to touch her, to try to bridge the distance between us. She believed the treatment they were offering would cure her. Was she disoriented and confused? The doctor hadn't used the sort of simple language that a brain being destroyed by cancer can comprehend.

Once again a team of medical staff offered suggestions of radical treatment. Radiotherapy, chemotherapy, eat this, exercise those muscles. When my aunt arrived, she drove a team of do-gooding occupational therapists out of the room. They were trying to teach her to stand, to walk. They were only doing their job. They infuriated me. What fucking planet were they on? Underneath the stream of expert opinion, my mother smiled bravely and I looked helplessly at my brother. She knew we needed her. She thought more time would mean she could help us, love us a little longer. I watched her wince as she turned her head on the pillow. More time was cruel.

∽

It seems that whenever I go into a bookshop there is a new account of miraculous survival in which the odds were beaten, where the impossible happened and the person lived. Among these survival stories are scattered a few accounts of death, such as Simone de Beauvoir's description of her mother's death in the 1960s or David Rieff's account of his mother Susan Sontag's encounter with cancer, first in the 1970s and then her death from the disease in 2004. Rieff's words challenge me. I wonder now, did we do the right thing in refusing treatment for my mother? All the medical team offered was experimental palliative care – a concept so confusing I had trouble grasping it. My mother was going to die, but they could keep her alive for a few more weeks, possibly a few months. But what would her quality of life be? What would those extra days look like?

Now I think my courage failed me. My husband's death had beaten me, in a way. I'd fought for his life and been defeated, effortlessly – cast aside by death – and I couldn't see the point in fighting anymore. When I read these accounts of people travelling the globe for miracle cures, stories of sustained self-belief in the face of medical certainty, I can't help thinking that perhaps my mother might have lived if I had dredged my soul for more courage, searched the medical establishments for an opinion that offered life instead of death.

The reality was something else. Her cancer was so swift it seemed to grow before our eyes. I would put my hand on her neck and feel it pulsing and multiplying beneath my fingers. Once she started the regime of chemotherapy, the cancer shrank as if contemplating defeat and then, in malevolent stillness, it sought her brain. The cancer mocked the chemicals, the science, the statistics, the doctors, and silently ate my mother up.

They told us there were worse cancers than the one that attacks the brain. They said she would sink into a coma. While she was awake, she would be confused. One moment we were talking of Christmas on the farm, away from the hospital, on the lawn under the trees. The next day she could barely move. Did our words drift to the stars and offend the gods with their desperate hope? The cancer stole everything in a matter of hours. We hadn't spoken, we hadn't had that moment to put all our fear into words. Once again, I hadn't been allowed to say goodbye.

I sat beside her until she was lucid. Waiting, wanting that moment where we could talk of her impending death. Does this sound crueller than 'more time'? Am I a monster to have forced my mother to the knowledge that there was no escape from the death she didn't want? I sat by her bed. My back went numb. My legs went to sleep. The hours passed. She slept and slept. Outside, the light tilted, deepened towards darkness. It pulled me from her bedside to stand and watch. Her movement brought me back. She smiled and saw me with nothing masking my face, saw my fear. I asked if she could remember what the doctors had said that morning. She couldn't recall seeing them. She asked me what they'd said.

What are you meant to do in such a moment? Who are you meant to be? Mother to your mother? I looked at her and knew her soul had always searched for truth. It roared up between us. She would live six more weeks and never again would we have a moment that sacred. Nothing hung between us and I gripped her hand. She knew, and I knew.

Now I question if I was cruel. I wonder if my mother really needed to know she was dying. I wonder if we really needed to talk about it, or if it was just me who needed this conversation. I comfort myself with the story of my mother breaking family ranks when my grandmother was dying of cancer. My mother said it was one of the hardest things she'd ever done, to tell her dying mother-in-law the truth. My grandmother had asked because she knew my mother would not lie to her. The bit of that story I remember most clearly was that my grandmother thanked my mother for her honesty. Everyone was angry at my mother, but she was peacefully defiant, sure she had been true to what this older woman had asked of her. My mother said we had a right to know we were going to die.

But now, on the other side, I think perhaps all I did was inflict more pain on a body that couldn't move without pain breaking over it.

∽

After my mother was dead I went into her room. Her body lay composed on the bed, but she wasn't there anymore. Thank

God. The terrible laboured breathing had stopped. There was just nothing.

I wanted her so badly. I wanted to be her child, to feel her hand on my head, hear her voice. The desire to mould my body to hers, to warm her with my life, was irresistible. I lay on her body. Lay on her stiff corpse. Mother, still. Motherless.

I stand in those slips of time outside the school gate, while people talk of their mothers slowly going mad. Of age creeping up on them, hips stiffening, eyes dimming, the TV turned up too loud. Nervous laughter escapes the group as the stories, somehow interchangeable, build around new levels of forgetfulness in their mothers. 'Oh,' they say, 'she sounds just like mine – forgetting people's names, getting the kids mixed up, leaving the oven on, the door unlocked, losing the car in the car park.'

These are lists I'm saved from making.

10

'Was it Ovid who said, There is so much wind here,
stones go blank.'

Anne Carson, *Decreation*

THE DAYS HAVE LENGTHENED. The kids play outside in the evenings after dinner. The world seems a milder place. I'm at odds
with this new mildness, with the softer beauty of spring, because
with each day the tension ratchets up. The end of summer means
the end of my leave without pay. I have to make a decision
about what comes next. I don't know what to do about this.
I can't face the beach, the heat; I don't want to swim, I don't
want to feel the sun on my face and legs. I don't want to have
Christmas, I'm tired of trying to make things fun.

I move through the day one task at a time and get the
house under control enough to go for a run. Slowly I'm
reclaiming my body, for who knew that his absence would

physically change the shape of me? I keep expecting people to comment. It's so obvious to me that my body announces his departure to the world. Friends must put my changed appearance down to my struggle to cope, or perhaps they just don't want to look too closely. But it's more primal than these explanations – quite simply, my body is different without him. Its boundaries have shifted; I no longer know where I start and finish. I used to be so physically confident. I used to feel powerful. But I've changed, and there are times when I feel so disconnected from who I used to be that I wonder whether I'll ever be comfortable in myself again. This body is as foreign to me as this life I'm living without him.

In a moment of pure escapism I book tickets for the kids and me to spend our summer in Europe. It's madness, but it means I have a whole other set of pressing tasks and decisions and can push down the really hard one. The end of the year slips by in a whirl of increasing heat and, though the effort of organising our itinerary, accommodation and packing is a chore, it feels easier than staying put.

We're ready to leave. We put the pony out in the paddock and say a teary farewell to him. He shrugs his head and turns to graze – he can't believe his luck at being in a big paddock. Our old dog will stay with my aunt and in the end we just shut the door behind us and, on a day when the heat is stinging the soles of our feet, I once again pack the kids in the car and we head to Sydney. But we don't stop there – we board a plane and after what seems an eternity, we arrive in London.

I recognise there is an element of insanity in choosing to take a three-year-old on a seven-week trip to Europe on my own, where it'll be winter, where there'll be no routine, much less freedom, and where he'll need constant entertainment. But somehow, in my head, it's simpler than facing the summer here.

It is cold when we get to London. We take the tube from the airport to University College, where we are to stay with a friend of mine, and as we walk up the stairs out of the underground, the cold hits me and the journey already seems worthwhile. The streets are lit with strings of lights; there are concrete and sirens and buildings with air dried of cold and moisture by heavy oil heaters. Our apartment is in a beautiful old building set in private gardens. The change couldn't be more complete. We go to sleep to the sound of the sirens and the reflection of flashing lights on the walls. I wonder if I should be angry with myself for taking my kids out of the safety of the country and placing them in the middle of a city which has recently, just down the road from where we are staying, suffered a horrendous terrorist attack. But it also feels right to be here and the novelty of a playground with brightly coloured play equipment is enough to make everyone happy, even if it makes me feel as though we've travelled halfway around the world to watch Charlie slide down a slippery dip.

My very dear friend is in London for two years working in a job for which I have a qualification. Though I'm tempted to apply for her position when it comes up again, I cannot imagine how I'd manage to do what she is doing and look after the kids. I realise I've already slipped a little bit away from the ambitious person I was only six months before. I seek no connections with her bosses, I don't feel the need to impress anyone at the centre where she works. Instead we just throw ourselves into Christmas. My friend has gone all out for us in her preparations: there's a huge Christmas tree and presents and welcoming meals and creative activities for the kids. She orders a turkey and I push down loneliness and try not to wish my brother was here with me. The kids don't notice a thing. Lottie, in particular, is entranced by all London offers. She goes ice skating, and wants to visit museums and art galleries and gaze at palaces and walk in famous parks. Charlie is not so entranced, and I know he would have been happier, and easier to handle, puddling around on the beach. But we push on.

We travel to Bristol to be met at the station by family friends who live in an old farmhouse in a village outside the city. My kids are captivated both by the larger-than-life Englishness of our host and the intrigue and mystery of the house. Charlie just wants to be held by this jolly Englishman, who is perhaps the largest man he's ever met. By the time I've dumped our bags and coats in the great hall, the kids have disappeared. In the kitchen the kettle is boiling on the Aga and there's a cat asleep on a chair under the kitchen table. Suddenly I'm exhausted and the relentlessness of the last two weeks rises in a small wave of tears. It's so good to be in a country kitchen, in a family big enough to absorb my small family. I could hide here for days. I pick up the cat and sit. I realise the last time I sat at this table was with my husband and we'd exchanged a secret smile.

These people embrace us. The kids climb all over them, all over their house and run through the winter woodlands that surround the garden. The family own two enormous

Anatolian shepherds. These are seriously huge dogs, bigger than a small pony. Everyone is worried my kids will be frightened of them, especially Charlie, who is much smaller than them. Instead he thinks they are the best dogs ever created. He shadows them through the house and garden and, apart from his broad Australian accent and the liberal scattering of freckles across his nose, he could be a model for little Lord Fauntleroy, as he lies in front of the coal fire snuggled into the warm side of the older of the two shepherds. In Bristol he is happy in a way he wasn't in London. He relaxes and stops being so hyperactive and difficult.

Neither of the kids wants to keep travelling and I find myself sharing the sentiment. What could France and Italy hold that could possibly be more wonderful than here? I arrange to come back and the thought of this home waiting for us on our return to the UK makes the next part of the trip seem possible.

We're back on the train to London. Charlie has become so independent. He trundles his Bob the Builder bag behind him up the station stairs and down onto the platform. We settle into the carriage and Lottie buries herself in her book while Charlie gets out his cars and trains and parks them on the tray in front of him. He drives them across the windows, down seats, along the floor and back again in a complicated pattern of highways, bridges and tunnels. I stare out of the window at the English countryside flashing by.

I hope the kids don't realise how hard I'm running from what I don't want to face. I hope, instead of desperation, they see independence and adventure. As we battle back through London peak hour on a bus filled with commuters, I wonder, not for the first time, at my reasoning abilities – how did I think this would be easier than a summer on the beach? But despite the schlepping, despite the crowds and the stress of travelling with kids, I am being renewed by the sight and sound of the world carrying on regardless of my loss.

In Paris we stay in a beautiful apartment with parquet floors and a sophisticated sound system perpetually threatened by Charlie's curious fingers. Out of the kitchen window is a view of the Eiffel Tower. It snows and all I want is to wander the streets, but the children chafe against the city and its heavy layer of sophistication and talk about home. They get into trouble for running on the grass and have no idea what they've done wrong. We haven't got long in Paris and it's both a relief and a source of frustration that we can't stay.

Italy is thick with frost, but much more like the country town we have left in Australia. In Italy we stay in a small village and follow the cows to pasture every morning, watch the pruning of the vines, crunch our way through the chestnut forest. Another friend meets us and we shop and cook and eat in tiny restaurants where there are no menus and the food is prepared in the family kitchen. Lottie tries everything with enthusiasm. Charlie eats pasta and cheese and fresh tomatoes and not much else, but no one cares. We don't want to leave Italy. Charlie loves that the naughtier and louder he is, the more delightful the Italians seem to find him. Italy saves us. It transforms our Continental trip into a joyous thing, it is everything I need it to be, and I realise that in many ways it is the closest in likeness to home.

We fly to Paris and catch the Eurostar back to London; then travel to Bristol, first to more friends of my parents.

They were particularly close to my mother and I'm touched by their fondness for her, their grief at her death and their desire to look after the kids and me. Finally, we return to the farmhouse outside Bristol. The kids greet it as if it were a second home. It is becoming clear to me that whatever the next year holds, it will be a difficult transition if I have to resettle my children into the suburbs.

When we get back to London, there is a phone call from my aunt and uncle. They, along with the university, the rest of my family and my friends have no real idea what I'm planning for the next year. They ring to say the retired couple who've been living in the cottage near the stables are moving out. Do I want to move into this bigger cottage when I get back? The house drops in my lap like a message from the gods. I don't think about work, or the consequences of not going back. I simply say, yes.

With that we pack our bags and go home.

11

WHEN WE COME BACK FROM EUROPE, I try.

To dodge the January days that burst from the inland earth like a nuclear reaction, we go to the coast before we head back over the mountains. But the day of our return, as if to mock my attempt at escape, is 45 degrees. We've come home to a summer that has most definitely not ended. I could weep, but it requires too much energy. Instead, I move through each day sweating, fighting the heat and the rising panic at my decision to resign from the university. We prepare to move down the hill and across the ram flat into the bigger cottage. I try to live as if life is not a daily risk.

This is the cottage in which my grandparents lived after they left the main house to make way for my aunt and uncle's growing family. It's only a small cottage, but it feels big with its high ceilings and airy rooms. The house is set back from the road and has a little porch that faces east, into which the sun pours every morning. My grandmother planted the garden when she moved in, and though it's been through innumerable tenants, there are still remnants of her in the placement of the trees. There's a lilac in the corner near the bedroom that flowers extravagantly and scents the house with its subtle perfume at the end of the day. There are plum trees, white cedars and a Chinese elm. Bare sticks lean wearily on wire trellises and I hope that with a little love and attention they'll grow and reveal themselves to be my grandmother's favourite climbing roses. There are more bare sticks outside the back door and they are all that remain of the magnificent wisteria that shaded the western side of the cottage in the summer and scented my dreams when I stayed here with my grandparents as a child.

Everything is stunted from lack of care. The retired couple who lived in the cottage for the past few years were incredibly tidy. They pruned back the garden till there was barely anything left. The glorious japonica, which used to hide the sewage tank, is now only three bare branches and will take years to recover. All around the edges of the cottage the ground is dead and hard like concrete. It's been repeatedly sprayed with chemicals, so not a skerrick of a weed would dare push its way through the almost-industrial wasteland.

On our first night back on the farm, after the kids are asleep, I walk down the hill and across the ram flat to paint the walls of what will become our new home. The familiar track is different at night. My ancient Jack Russell, Daniel Dog, who has happily survived our absence, trots ahead, delighted to be out and about when the heat has gone from the day. There's no wind tonight to blow the cooling air from the flat up the hill, so my skin prickles as I climb the gate, slip under the electric fence and through a layer of coolness rising from the extra moisture on the flat. We walk up the hill to the quiet cottage. I open the door and move through the empty rooms, climb the ladder and start painting the walls of the sewing room. This is the room I slept in as a child. Tonight, with its windows open to catch any passing breath of wind, the room smells just as it did when I was small. I move to the window and swing the gauze screen open. Standing, my elbows propped on the windowsill, I breathe in the heady scent of freshly cut hay. The night swirls with possibilities. I feel a long way from London and winter.

We move in and make the cottage our home. The kids love it and so do I. We're much nearer the sheds and stables, and the action of the farm is just over the back fence. Life feels busier. The cottage doesn't have the same sort of isolation and peace as the big house on the hill, but there is still a concrete slab out the back on which to place a table and a barbecue, and sit and watch the sun drop over the hill in the evenings. The garden quickly loses its tidy look as bikes, dogs, balls of every description litter the grass. I cart wheelbarrows of manure and tip it all over the concrete-like dirt. It looks messy. I wonder if anything, ever, will grow out of that hard, poisoned ground.

All my furniture arrives from Sydney. I write my letter of resignation. I book Charlie into preschool and two days a week he catches the school bus from the end of the driveway with Lottie. I wave them goodbye and wonder what I do next.

∽

When I stand outside the angst about my career, I can see this was the only sensible decision. But letting go of my job feels like a major risk. The arguments against resigning cycle through my head.

'Surely now, more than ever, it's important to hold down a full-time job.'

'Perhaps if I employed a housekeeper . . .'

'Perhaps if we moved closer to the university . . .'

'Perhaps if I dropped to part time . . .'

'If I leave now, I'll never climb back on the career ladder.'

'If I walk away, I'll be forgotten and all my hard work will have been for nothing.'

'I'll become defined by my kids and never have an independent identity.'

'If I resign, he'll have stolen my career as well as everything else.'

I creep around the nature of the problem and, even though the decision has been made and I've resigned, the arguments and insecurities still cripple me. What my children need is a parent not constantly distracted by work; they need less activity and more space; they need to be out here. Against the obviousness of this, my job glitters. No matter the chaos of my private life, I could turn and admire my workplace self. I could measure my worth against the comments of the students who took my classes, congratulate myself at having gained the prize of a teaching position at a big university.

To leave this behind, even for a short time, feels terrifying. Who am I if I am not an historian, a lecturer at university? Who am I if I don't have students knocking on my door? Who am I if I don't have the reassurance of colleagues seeking my opinion on their work? Without the surety of my work, the blessed miracle of having a decent sum of money deposited in my bank account every week, will I become directionless, anonymous, invisible?

Then, as so often happens when there is a space or doubt in your life, I get a follow-up phone call from my publisher about the project we'd talked of during my trip to Melbourne. Was I still interested in a commission to write another history book? The commission is generous, far more than the book will ever make out of royalties. The money would be enough to live on up here for a year or so, and the promise of publication instantly diminishes my insecurities about leaving my job. I fly to Melbourne, sign on the dotted line and return home with direction and piles and piles of photocopies to read through.

The book is to showcase the State Library of Victoria's collection of documents, manuscripts, letters and diaries written by the men and women who'd settled the Western District. I will select and arrange the material, finding the characters whose words manage to evoke something of life on the frontier, and write an introduction.

With a project to complete, my weeks develop something of a routine. On the days Charlie goes to preschool, I sit at my computer, or out on the porch, photocopies in hand, and immerse myself in the world of the early settlers. On the days Charlie is home, we work in the garden, or go out on the farm. One day a week he packs his backpack and spends the day with my aunt and uncle. Usually this means the morning out on the farm with my uncle and the afternoon working in the garden with my aunt. He returns at the end of the day with potatoes he's dug, or tomatoes he's picked and stories of his great usefulness.

From above I look down as a slick of oil once more covers the secret life of my grief.

12

YESTERDAY THE PHONE RANG EARLY. It was the neighbours calling to tell us a new foal had been born last night. I could hear the excited tone in their daughter's voice as she spoke to Lottie. I was making lunches, but the acute awareness of new life changed the morning. We headed up the road and piled onto the back of the ute, school bags and uniforms getting covered in dust as we jolted across the paddock. The mare's fine, thoroughbred head turned towards us. She stood over her crumpled baby, who sheltered underneath her. Her udder was hot and swollen, and the baby nuzzled into her flank, trying to find the source of the sweet scent of milk. The kids were all quivering excitement, trying to be quiet and not upset the new mother, but their voices singing out as they argued about names. The morning suddenly felt fresh and clean, even as the heat rose. Dust swallowed our vehicle on its way back down the track.

When I think about death, I have to force myself also to

think about life. Sometimes I feel like a snake shedding an old skin. I can't work out whether I wear my grief on me like a second layer, or whether it's a skeleton shaping me from the inside out. In moments of hope, I feel my body breaking out. It feels raw and vulnerable to face the world and I wonder if, like that snake, I will shed my wounded skin each year. With each season, what has come before oozes up. Can those around me smell it? Its stench is so heavy I can taste it in my mouth. It tastes like fear. Even on a day of birth, an autumn morning when the poplar leaves turn the line of the creek to a golden road, a morning when a thoroughbred baby takes her first breath, it sits metallic on my tongue.

I always find it hard to let go of winter, so I embrace the first signs of its return. The trees drop their leaves with relief after their long battle with the heat of summer. It's the withdrawal of it, the quietness of the birds leaving, the sinking down of the sap, the hardness of the soil; the easiness of my own company, the long evenings in front of the fire. I walk underneath the freezing night sky and the stars are brighter in the frost.

I'm reading Robert Dessaix's *Night Letters*, and his description of solitude catches at the edge of my panic – 'any passing phantom can sink its teeth into your throat' when you are alone. But solitude feels easier in winter. It's easier to dress up my loneliness, my abandonment, my desertion in the short days and cold nights.

There is a single lamb in the paddock beside the garden. Her companions have been shipped off in a truck and she's been left behind, 'saved', because she was fly-struck. She is on her own and doesn't feel like she's been saved. She calls all day and night. I worry about her as she strains against her isolation. She startles easily and runs to the end of the paddock to be as far away from the activity in the garden as she can get. In the evening, she creeps towards the water trough for a drink. She must be parched as she has called all day. But the water trough is near the garden and the garden is filled with running children and barking dogs. Her need for water overcomes her fear and I watch her creep in.

As the days turn into weeks she settles into her aloneness. She still calls if she sees the big flock over on the hill or if the rams wander up the flat across the other side of the road. But mostly she is settled and her attention becomes tuned to the house, to the slam of the back door, the sound of the phone ringing, the different noises that mark the movement of the day. Her adaptation is surprisingly swift. I watch her marking the boundaries of her days and I wonder why I can't be as adaptive and turn my loneliness into solitude.

I should say that I do still have a companion. He is short and old and completely obsessed with his own self-importance. He snores loudly at night and shares my impatience when the children won't go to bed on time. His favourite time of the day is when, at last, we close their bedroom door. He supervises dinner (closely), story-time less attentively, and heaves a sigh of relief when I throw myself on the couch at the end of the day. He settles for an evening of trashy TV, maybe the tasty morsel of a good book or perhaps a long phone conversation. It doesn't matter; as long as I'm on the couch, he can relax. His presence pushes against the stalking loneliness.

Daniel Dog was a piece of my husband as well – he was

his dog first. When my husband died, I became the centre of Daniel Dog's world, just as I became the centre for my children. But the dog is different. He's self-sufficient, nothing like a child; better still, he doesn't hold a grudge if I lose my temper or trample him during the busyness of the day. He needs very little attention, all he asks is that he may be near me. He doesn't like to be petted, he doesn't want to sit on me; he just likes to be able to see me.

I ran him over shortly after we left Sydney. I'm not sure how he got under the car – there was a confusion of barking dogs and perhaps he was snapped at by one of the others, but under the wheel he went. I felt a bump and pulled up to find him struggling like a squashed beetle. I made him a bed near the fire and thought, he won't make it. After a sleepless night, I got up in the morning and I couldn't find him anywhere. Eventually I tracked him to a bush outside the door. We took him to the vet, and all the way into town I talked the kids through the fact that he'd had a good life, that it was much more merciful to put him to sleep if he was in pain and the vet couldn't fix him. We finally reached the surgery and tenderly carried him inside. I felt like one of my limbs was about to be cut off. But then the vet examined him and could find nothing broken – just a poor, sore, squashed Jack Russell who would be back in action in a couple of days.

So, miraculously, he survived! I ran him over in a huge stationwagon, this ancient Jack Russell, who has already survived a dose of rat poison, three days stuck down a rabbit hole and a serious mauling from a bull terrier. My husband didn't, my mother didn't, but the dog did. The episode makes me realise that when Daniel Dog does die, a whole history of my life will go with him. I quietly brace myself against the day when I will have to say goodbye to him again.

∾

In deference to the anxiety expressed by my friends and family that I might sink into a well of loneliness and never be heard from again, I join a tennis group. My father is pleased. Although he's led an independent life in Melbourne since his marriage to my mother broke up, he's always on the end of the phone making sure I'm still standing upright. A tennis group reassures him that I'm not becoming a recluse.

It's made up of ladies mostly of my mother's generation, though some are much older. When I first moved out here, Tuesday tennis was the one form of social contact I attended without anxiety. Most of these ladies knew my mother and grandmother. They know my story. I have friends who find this sort of generational knowledge claustrophobic. They say that they cannot break free of their family; they are always being compared to an aunt, a grandmother, a great-grandmother. For me, after the anonymity of the city, where everyone is a stranger, this knowledge feels like a comfy pair of slippers into which I slip, named and known.

Tuesday tennis becomes part of my weekly routine. In the morning I make an extra sandwich and after Charlie and I see off the school bus, we walk home, pack our lunch and drive to someone's house, where I play tennis on ant-bed courts and my son is looked after by a bevy of ladies, all experienced in the ways of small boys. In this way we are reacquainted with the district; between them these women know everything that is going on. I'm welcomed onto green lawns. We lunch under old shade trees and explore beautiful gardens, each reflecting the personality of its owner. In many ways it's a privileged world, but it's also a world in which people work hard. There are no city-soft hands out here. In this eclectic group of women I find solace. It's their essential femaleness, their knowledge of cooking, gardening and raising kids, mixed with years of living on the land, that make them a source of comfort and practicality.

I have other older women in my life. Two wonderful women, both writers, both of my mother's generation or thereabouts, come for a working break from the city. They bring the wide reach of their intellects into my physical world. Both of them have only known me in the cloistered university world of lecture halls, seminar rooms, cafés and bookshops. Neither of them knew my husband. Later, they write to me separately to tell me something has shifted from my body.

We walk together across the ram flat and watch Lottie ride her chestnut pony round in circles. She has become passionate about riding. Every afternoon after school she changes into jeans and walks to the stables, where she saddles Will and rides down to the ram flat to practise the movements she'll perform at the weekend competitions we've started attending. Poor old Will is happy to oblige her desire to jump anything she can, and to circle endlessly in pursuit of the perfection she has read about in books borrowed from the library. But really her enthusiasm has reached the limits of his ability.

As we stand together watching her struggling to perform movements that are beyond the stiffness of Will's old joints,

I realise I am going to have to get her a new horse. This is a daunting thought, for I trust Will with her; I know she can handle him, I know she's safe. A new horse though . . . First there is the drama of finding the thing, then the anxiety of watching my small child forge a relationship with a new animal; so much can go wrong and it's for these reasons that I've been putting off admitting that Lottie has outgrown old Will.

I will take my problem to tennis next week – someone will know of a horse and, even if they don't, they will share my anxiety at the transition from first to second pony.

We wander back up to a dinner of roast lamb, killed and butchered for me by my uncle. We eat potatoes, pumpkin, parsnips, broccoli and broad beans, all from my aunt's garden, and talk of books and the importance of work to a full life. It feels luxurious to have the attention of these women; to have them as witnesses to what I'm trying to create up here and to the fact that, if just for a minute, things are a whole heap better than they were when I left Sydney.

We talk into the night and they tease me about the possibility of new love, of a future with another man. I go to bed warm with their companionship, content also for them to hold the possibility of a relationship for me in their imaginations, for I have no room for it in mine. Perhaps solitude is beginning to accompany me lightly; certainly sorrow has drained me of desire. So if I find myself looking over the fence at other lives, or dreaming of the man who has left me here on my own, I am slowly learning that if I stand still long enough, the tempest will recede.

13

MY MOTHER WAS A COUNTRY GIRL caught in the city through circumstance, through choice, through opportunity.

My mother loved ducks. She loved their sleek, shiny suits. She loved their self-important waggle and the way they cocked their heads to peer at you with their penny-pricked eyes. She collected wooden ducks and, beautifully painted, elegantly formed, they marched across our coffee table, ushering their family of ducklings. In a quiet moment, her granddaughter would be allowed to play with them. My mother never really went for the country-craft version of the duck. She liked her ducks realistically rendered.

Since we moved into the cottage, I've been looking after the chooks. It's a job I enjoy. I've always wanted them at the end of my garden and I'm not surprised to find that I'm more interested in the noises they make, their hierarchy and personalities, than in their eggs. Don't get me wrong – the eggs are wonderful. Fresh and so yellow when they're cooked that they change the taste of everything I put them in. So I try to focus on their utility, but I get distracted by the way the ladies cluster at my feet when I appear at the back gate. I get distracted by the way they sprint from the hayshed, from behind the stable, from way up the back of the machinery paddock, when they hear the back door slam at a certain time of day.

The kids name all the hens and the special roosters who have somehow managed to escape my uncle's crockpot. We have one rooster, Snappa, a bantam, who comes up to my ankle. He blusters and blarneys his way around the farmyard. He will line you up and leap at you if you turn your back on him, but if you happen to spot him as he charges towards you, he will screech to a halt and pretend to be on an important errand in some other direction. He is a wonderful babysitter as he keeps my inquisitive son in the garden. If it wasn't for Snappa patrolling the back gate, I would have many more heart-stopping moments. While Snappa struts his stuff, I know Charlie won't be tempted to go and play on the tractor, in the wool shed, in the hay shed, chook shed, cow byre, ram shed or lambing shed – all the myriad play possibilities safely limited till he is accompanied by his big sister past the patrolling, pocket-sized rooster.

Then we're given ten ducklings from a neighbour up the road. For the first week they live in a big cardboard box in the garage under a light. They quickly outgrow this temporary set-up and the kids spend hours preparing the end of the chook shed for them. When all is ready, they take up the box and release them into the yard. They've blown up an old paddling pool and built ramps in and out. Then they sit and watch as the ducklings skid round the edges of the pool, snapping at flies.

The ducklings grow alarmingly quickly – their ability to convert food into body mass makes me appreciate why ducks are a staple in many countries. The kids and my uncle spend a satisfying half day constructing a duck gate in the garden and giving them their own water trough to surf. I come home to the sight of ducks grazing on a bright green lawn; ducks tucked up asleep in the deep shade of a shrub.

I'm amazed at how different they are to the chooks. All the advice I've had on keeping ducks is to treat them like chooks. They are as like chooks as the sun is to the moon. The chooks are quick and darting, independent and aloof, even from each other. The 'quackers', as I've taken to calling them, work in a pack; they get upset if they are separated. They are party ducks. They make the chooks look like staid old committee ladies, uptight and regular in their ways. I come out at night, drawn by the moon and the scent of lucerne in the air, and there they are surfing their trough, taking a little moonlight dip before bed. The chooks go to bed as soon as dusk starts to fall, they ruffle their feathers in disapproval of the rowdy ducks at the end of the shed. The chooks scatter at the first sign of rain or of wind heralding a storm. They head for the big shed and won't come out till all is calm again. The ducks flap their delight at the pouring rain. They paddle from puddle to puddle and then find a pool in the middle of the round yard. They skid across the surface. From the shelter of the stable I can hear the ladies fussing at such disgraceful conduct.

My mother loved ducks and hated committee ladies and I want to tell her these things. I want her to know that I'm doing this; I'm bringing up the kids, surrounding them with life. I want more than anything to hear her tell me I'm being the best mother I can be. I want her advice on everything from how to make white sauce to how to deal with the fragile self-image of a rapidly developing daughter. In the mornings, as I mix up the duck food and bang it into the trough, I want her to see this new version of me. I want her to see me out in the early morning dressed in my workers – there's no computer, no funky clothes, no deadlines or child drop-offs, no lecture to prepare, papers to mark, seminar to attend – only the ducks to feed. But no matter how I try to conjure her to witness my transformation, she will not appear.

My uncle is given another thirty young ducks. They have been kept in a tiny cage and they don't really know how to walk. They arrive in a crate on the back of the ute and are so exhausted with terror that they can barely stand – they keep flopping onto their bellies, prone, until a new wave of adrenalin breaks over them.

We chase them into the end of the chook shed and go about making them comfortable. They are so unused to people that they stampede away from me as I open the gate to give them fresh feed and water. Someone only has to walk past their pen and they panic and run over the top of each other.

Our old ducks come up to the fence quacking their greeting. We let them in with the young ones to try to settle them down. The old ducks cruise the water trough in the corner of the yard, unruffled by my presence. I hope they will show the newcomers the joy of a dip in the water, or the pleasure of grazing on the green grass under the pepper trees, or on the edges of the hay shed where the gutter leaks. We leave them all shut up together for a week or so, until the new ducks settle into their home.

In the mornings I swing open the big door at the end of the shed and out comes a great melee of ducks. There are so many they swamp the chooks with their quacking. They move in a herd like sheep and are at first indistinguishable from each other. Most of them are Welsh harlequins, though we have a smattering of khaki campbells and the odd crossbreed mallard. They gradually sort themselves into distinct groups. Mostly there are one or two drakes with six or so ducks. As soon as the door to the shed opens in the morning the herd breaks into its separate groups and waddles off to their favourite parts of the farm. They are not territorial, as such – that is, they won't fight each other for space – but the drakes will try to rape any unwary duck who crosses their path and is not in their group. They form close ties and, if separated from their companions, both ducks and drakes quack with great intensity until they find each other again.

There is one couple in whom I am fascinated. He's a beautiful Welsh harlequin with a smart white band around his neck. But he's not a big duck, just pretty. She's a little plain mallard cross, whom I call Penelope, as she is always trying to save herself for her husband. She isn't like the pure Welsh harlequins who are dressed in maidenly white, speckled through with brown, grey and green. Instead, she's a dull brown all over. But for some reason the older drakes, who are huge in comparison to Penelope's small, neat mate, are obsessed with her. Every morning when I open the door of the chook house, there is a great commotion as Penelope and her husband try to escape to their sanctuary behind the stables. The big drakes seek out Penelope and chase her – she's faster and lighter, but they're stronger. Often they catch and rape her, and then her little husband tries to rescue her by pushing the big drakes off his mate. It is pitiful and clumsy, in a very ducky way, and I'm always interfering and chasing the big ducks off so the couple can escape.

During the day, they hang out down in the old ram shed, which is a fair way from where the dogs are tied up. They're always the last home in the evening, and wait till right on dark before sneaking into the shed.

Then one day the little duck comes back without her mate. I've seen a fox lurking a few paddocks away from the ram shed and he must have got game enough to snatch the little drake during the day. Penelope is bereaved, and without any protection from the big drakes, her life becomes hellish. She tries to attach herself to a little group of five ducks and two drakes. Their territory is much more sedate – they hang out behind the stable and in the cow paddock, but never venture very far from the safety of the dogs. When she first approaches them, they hiss and turn on her if she comes too close, but, out of loneliness and desperation, she persists and tags along a few metres behind them.

As the days go on, she gradually becomes part of the group and the drakes started to offer her some protection from the three big drakes who preyed on her. After about two weeks, she is a firmly established part of her new group. Life is safer for her now – she's not harassed nearly as much – but every time I see her, I wonder if she hankers for her days of freedom and risk with her mate down at the ram shed.

14

I SHOULD BE READING JANE CAVERHILL'S JOURNAL. I've been waiting for it to arrive from the State Library of Victoria, hoping it will be the woman's voice needed in the book I'm writing to balance the men's triumphant tales of conquest and empire-building. But instead I've been studying horse-sale catalogues. Who knew there was such a national market for leisure horses? There is one magazine, a veritable bible for anyone wanting to buy or sell a horse, which is almost as thick as the Yellow Pages. A friend comes over and we work our way through its ads. Anything close by and reasonably priced seems to have sold the minute the magazine hit the newsagency. We expand our search, but after a futile few hours on the phone, my friend heads home. I get dinner on, chop wood, shut up the chooks and ducks and supervise Lottie's riding. I help her rug Will and we dish up a big feed for him. Since she's been riding him so much, I've had to start feeding him grain. Every morning after Lottie puts him in his paddock, she brings down a saucepan full of barley and I leave it on the stove to soak through the day. Will can't believe his luck, but if I didn't feed him, there is no way he would be able to do what she is asking of him. He tucks his head into the feed bin and the two of us stand there listening to his happy snuffling.

Later that evening, my friend rings to say that she's been going back through some old magazines and thinks she has found a potential horse for Lottie. Only trouble is, it's in Victoria, which is a long way for me to take any advisors. It's not impossible, though, as I'm heading down south to the Western District for a research trip at the end of the month. My friend rings the woman and, by some miracle, the horse we are interested in hasn't sold. The woman sends me a DVD of the little mare. I watch it over and over. There is something about her swinging trot, her willingness to poke along quietly, but still with a cadence, that suggests untapped potential. But, I caution myself, she is everything we're not looking for – a mare and a thoroughbred, and an ex-racehorse. I'd wanted a gelding, a stockhorse of some description, nothing flash, just reliable and with a bit of ability. But I can't get this mare out of my head.

My wanting reminds me what else I'm feeling now. I'm frustrated at the inertia holding me tight. Tiny spiders drop from the sky. Their webs drift, catch on bare branches, shift like silver traces. They're meant to signal moisture, another sign of rain coming. But I can't see it. If anything, the atmosphere is drier, more charged. The wind is relentless, the spiders drift and the stock won't settle. Through the window I watch them stride the boundary of the homestead paddock. The wind ripples the surface of memory, tears at careful stitches.

Moments of loss merge into each other until they form a tangled mass. I try to tease them apart so each may be dealt with individually. I think, if I could see each one separately then I wouldn't be so easily overwhelmed. But they loop and curl round each other so that one begins before the other ends. They are slippery like blood and I fight to remember what happened, when and where. The past, when it rises, must be approached with caution – stealthy, anaesthetised caution.

These moments arrive from some depthless place, which is disconcerting. Just as I think I'm able to embrace the future, just as it looks as if my world is expanding, I'll be swamped by a memory so stubborn that if I don't turn from the present to face it, I'll remain trapped.

∽

Hospital again. I braced myself for what I'd see. I drove past the place where I found my husband after he'd run away the first time. I carefully parked the car and pushed back the memory of my mother's support. She'd driven with me to find him, the two of us wide-eyed with shock at the places he was taking us. We'd taken him home and sat with him while he shook and trembled. I walked quickly past the place and shrank like a fox caught in a spotlight. My stomach curled at the memory, and also at what I was to face in the hospital. Without my husband. Though he intrudes, he's not what this memory is about.

My mother was curled on her side. A doctor took a sample of her spinal fluid to be tested, and I coughed and coughed and could not stop throwing up. I forced myself to sit in the chair next to her. She was asleep, always asleep, and I sat and marvelled at the curve of her back, at her vulnerability, at the swiftness of this disease. Then I went and stood in the corridor with my younger brother and we held each other and wept, and he sheltered me and I tried to hold him too. But my back was bowed. We wiped our eyes, stifled our howls and I tried to remember where I'd left my children.

It was always like this. The logistics of getting through the day kept getting in the way of what was happening to my mother. Now she is gone, those last days keep haunting me and I grow frustrated because I can't find my way to her side.

My grief for my mother is open and raw and honest. It rises quickly to the surface, unbidden. But it's also complicated because it becomes entangled with him. Of course, I still fight to be free from her, for she remains the measuring stick in my head, the magnetic north against which I line up my emotions. I worry at the shortcuts I take, at the morally ambiguous decisions over which I know she would confront me. I worry my children are growing up without her strong guidance. I worry about how much less of a person I am without her. Her absence presses on me, changes my shape, changes my children's future and, even as I acknowledge this, I'm forced to face the question of why I feel so differently about her death. Why does it feel so different to lose someone from suicide and someone from cancer? They are both dead, they have both left me alone. They were both terribly ill. At the last, they both fought for life. Neither of them died easily. Neither of them died nicely. But how I feel about each one is so different as to be an almost separate experience.

Separate is how they should be – I should mourn them separately. But their deaths are intertwined and I can't find my way into one moment without being ambushed by another. I start off being angry with my husband and end up missing my mother – neither emotion is resolved and each displaces the other.

The wind has got under my mind. It works away at my head and buzzes around until it finds something to prise loose. My thoughts flap like a piece of corrugated iron on the roof. Not rhythmically, but violently. I abandon all attempts at reading Caverhill's memoir, which has at last arrived. I'm as restless as the stock and pace the boundaries of the house. These are the days when it's hard to believe things will get better. When C. S. Lewis wrote about grief he also wrote about his crisis of faith. He was confused that his loss was causing him to question the precise principles that he thought would anchor him through such sorrow. In turn, I wonder how one death can cause me to lose faith and another death seems only to confirm that there has to be some sort of natural order to life, some all-controlling being, some God.

∞

It seems to take us a long time to realise that our bodies are mortal.

When we were climbing in Alaska, I felt confronted by my singular lack of importance, by the sheer size of the landscape. I don't know whether he got this quite as much. Maybe it was because his body was so much stronger than mine, his very maleness somewhere at its core refused to acknowledge his vulnerability. But as we walked through that landscape, I went to sleep each night wondering if we would be crushed by snow and ice. I woke each morning and wondered if the rock would fall and carry me into the underground rivers roaring beneath the glacier. As I walked through each day in a state of controlled panic, somewhere, at some point, I suddenly 'got' my insignificance. There was no superstructure around me to rescue me from death. Nothing would save me if the mountain fell. I could be carefully intelligent about the minute-by-minute decisions – where to place my foot, where to pitch our tent, where to place the protection that tied us to the face of the mountain – but mostly I had to live with the pure chance of life and death.

That's what it felt like when my mother died. Pure fucking bad luck. It happens. We die all the time. Some of us die quicker than others. Some of us have heart attacks, some of us have strokes, some of us get cancer, some of us get run over. But we all die by chance. By that, I mean we don't see it coming. We can take precautions, but for our daily survival we must push our mortality to the back of our minds. My mother getting cancer felt like the mountain falling. It was nothing personal, she was just in its way. But with him, it felt personal. It felt deliberate. There was a choice and he chose to go away. I carry him – his memory, his voice, his skin, his eyes – in my body. But it's a heavy burden, because though I want to mourn him purely, his choice robs me of that ability. If it were the reality of nature that took him away, then perhaps I would walk through each day differently. Perhaps he wouldn't weigh me down so that I don't have to choose to swim away.

Then I tell myself that he didn't feel as though he had a choice. That he kept walking to the edge and throwing himself off not to be rescued, but because he felt nature had let him down, that he was alive when he should be dead.

I don't know, because I lost him long before he could talk to me, to anyone, with any truth about that moment when he would hurl himself over. But he always chose places where he could, possibly, be rescued. Where there was a chance that fate, that something, that God? would step in and say, NO, you will live.

But there are only so many times that can happen. Did he think that if he took himself to the very edge, it would shock him out of the place he was in? Did he think that if he looked death in the face, he could return to life and choose to live? Didn't he realise out there on the mountain with me that death is greedy – it takes the weak, it takes anyone who gives it an inch? Death is hungry: even though it knows it will have us all in the end, it wants us now. He went again and again to death. Could he be so surprised that it claimed him eventually? Am I?

The way I see the world has been challenged by his absence. Because, in the end, nothing was strong enough to make him hold onto life – not my love, not my faith, not our kids – nothing could hold the past back from claiming him once again, swallowing him up into darkness. I write in silence so that I can hear any defence he offers, any explanation that will leap to the page as I take him and pin him to a board and demand of him the answers he couldn't give me when he lived. But all I hear is the empty echo of his absence.

A few days after watching the DVD of the mare, I pack

the car and, with defiance, drive my children to Victoria, where we ride the horse. I look at my daughter – she never knew riding could feel like this, the mare is so powerful, so free in her paces, so light compared to heavy old Will. Her name is Belle, she blows a careful breath over me and I know she looks like risk. Her head is finely chiselled, her eyes are gentle, but everything about her speaks of good breeding, of quality. She's so sensitive her skin crawls when a strange hand touches her.

Though my husband's parents have given me some money for a new horse, if I buy this mare for my daughter it will be a brave thing. I tell the woman I'll think about it and we get back in the car and keep driving. We head into Melbourne and stay with my father. I show him the DVD and, as always, he's coolly rational – he can't see the difficulty in the decision. The mare looks lovely, goes quietly, is the right price – where's the problem? If she doesn't work out, I can sell her on. He's right and he's wrong. I tell him I'll sleep on it. He raises his eyebrows.

The next morning we're on the road early to start my research trip. I tell the kids we're following the road the first settlers took out of Melbourne as they made their way west to find the promised land of Australia Felix. I give them a map each and a list of place names where the major characters in the book I'm writing settled. One of them, Niel Black, has become the centrepiece of the book. His journal is full of intensity, of his experience, his acute observations and a dry Scottish sense of humour. In 1839, he rode his horse out of Melbourne to find out for himself if there was any truth behind the rumours of a land flowing in milk and honey.

I plan to follow his journey. We drive out of Melbourne, through Geelong, then, like Black, head across the flat plain to find the mysterious shape of Mount Elephant looming in the distance.

I want to gather my impressions around me as I drive. The words of one of my first history lecturers come to me – he said the most important item in any historian's repertoire was a strong pair of boots. He was asking us not to disregard the need to walk over the landscape in order to understand what else documents hold besides words. For, in the austere surroundings of the archives, it's easy to forget the effect of the dust, heat or bone-crunching cold in which those words were written.

So we explore the Western District, criss-crossing our tracks so that the map looks like an Aboriginal dot painting. One night we stay on the coast and go to sleep to the sound of crashing waves. The next day we drive to the foot of the Grampians and have lunch beneath their brooding bulk. The kids travel easily now and I catch my breath on a taste of freedom. After a week we head back to the Murray River and then drive out onto the flat plains which Thomas Mitchell crossed to find Australia Felix. In Narrandera, sitting under the jacarandas, I ring the woman and buy the mare.

15

THE MARE ARRIVES. She's lost weight since we last saw her and she's fractious and suspicious. But our family seems bigger and braver. We lead her down the lane and put her in the paddock. She's had a long trip to get here and when the halter is taken off, she explodes in a cacophony of movement. She gallops so fast that I fear she won't be able to stop before she hits the fence. But as I watch her circle the paddock, I realise that although she's snorting like a freight train, she's still in control. She flies past me and then pulls up in three short strides, before wheeling away and taking off again. She gallops until she's in a lather of sweat. I decide to put old Will in with her. I take off his halter and he trots off, full of interest in this new companion. She squeals and wants him to play. He puts his head down at the unaccustomed abundance of green feed and becomes a solid grazing machine. She settles and starts grazing next to him. I turn and walk back up the lane.

Winter is closing in and I haven't seen my closest friends since we returned from overseas. One is London-based, another lives in Melbourne and the third in Sydney. We've known each other for more than a decade and these friendships have helped me through the worst of the last few years. A Sydney conference gives us an excuse to catch up, and we've arranged to meet. I drive the familiar road back over the mountains.

We meet for breakfast by the beach, then head to the Korean Baths in Kings Cross. These baths have been a favourite retreat since we were poverty-stricken PhD students who had plenty of time but no money. We'd pay our entry and spend the day there, alternating between the sitting room (where there was free tea and coffee) and the baths, where conversations took on an intensity that comes with the intimacy of bathing together.

In this hidden female place I squat and scrub beneath the shower, and something of my reserve is sloughed off. Entering the baths returns me to a simpler time. Then our conversation flowed around the vagaries of supervisors, the complexity of relationships, our first experiences of tutoring at university, the difficulties we were having with our writing and the insecurities and dreams we harboured for our futures. Death did not slide under any of these moments.

Now we're all working, the luxury is being here together. We can afford a massage. After we shower and loll in the baths, a Korean woman strides into the room and calls my number. I follow her and she motions me onto the massage table. My identity is stripped, along with my clothes, and almost blissfully I embrace the anonymity of being naked. The room is full of slabs of female flesh. I'm doused in warm water, wrapped in warm towels, pummelled, pushed and most divinely touched.

Why do I think the hands that run over my back can feel his absence? Does it sound strange that neutral hands, indifferent hands, trace the shape of my desire? My body misses him in a craven way. It's not tormented by deceit, by hope turned sour, as my mind is – my body simply desires. In this desire I am trapped, duplicitous. Duped by my own body.

There is so much hurt, so much that can't be said anymore, so many unfinished conversations. One of the hardest things has been to shield others from the anger he lit in me. People expect grief in the form of tears, they expect softness and vulnerability, and I can't seem to show that I know I'm not performing my grief *properly*. I know people want me to fall in pieces so they can comfort me. And it's not as if I don't want rescuing – I do – but I can't seem to give in to the expressions of missing him that people apparently feel they need to see. Instead, they see me going to work, leaving my children, *coping well*. I want to shout at them as well as at him. Because I know he knew how much I loved him. He knew I gave my love freely, innocently – and it almost saved him. In the end it couldn't, but that didn't stop me from giving till I had nothing left to give, and even then he couldn't resist taking a little more, though he knew he shouldn't, though he hated himself for it.

∽

Back home, winter bites. I put on a jumper against the chill of the falling frost, shove my feet in boots and head up to the stables to check the horses. The dogs are curled tight in their log kennels, their chains clink in the freezing air as they lift their heads and watch me pass. The moon is bright; its shadows trap the familiar shapes of the farmyard in an eerie glow. When we lived on the coast, the movement of the moon pulled at the tide. It rose over the back of the eastern headland and its presence would draw me onto the deck to listen to the waves. On the cliff above the sea, the air would feel tight as the moon tipped this body of water higher up the beach.

In Alaska we slept on the edge of the ocean in that in-between space separating the forest from the sea. I would fall asleep afraid the moon would pull the ocean right into our tents. But out here the moon is different. If anything, it feels more powerful, capable of turning night into day, and I often wonder if it's because there is no water to dilute its pulling power. Out here I can feel my body swayed by the cycle. Tonight, when the moon is full, I'll sleep lightly. Under the falling frost, I shut in the chooks and ducks and throw a biscuit of hay to a hungry Will and an indifferent Belle. The moon sits low in the sky. I crawl into bed and pull the woollen quilt around my ears. The air is cold to breathe.

But sleep doesn't bring peace, instead a dream returns. We're in Alaska. We're out at sea, and somehow we're in the water together – we're in trouble. I'm not panicking: in the dream I know we can make it back to the beach, though it seems to be rapidly pulling away from us. We're caught in a strong rip, but I can see where we could swim out of it. This is strange in itself because he was the one who could read the sea and I was the one who was blind to it.

I am holding him; I am confused – he's the stronger swimmer and he's bigger than I am, yet I'm holding him. He won't relax and float on his back. Adrenalin starts to pump through me. I know I'm in the dream, but I can't get out, and I can't get him to just float on his back. If he floated then someone might be able to rescue us. But he panics and his panic is blind and wild. He pushes me down, holds me under the water and stands on me to get a breath, to get above the sea. I am struggling to get out from under him, struggling to push him away from me. I am pushing him to his death. I know this, yet I kick and strike blindly at him. 'You stupid idiot!' I scream, but no sound comes as my lungs fill with water. All he has to do is swim, which is like breathing to him. SWIM. I watch him struggle as the rip carries him away from me. I strike out for the beach and make it easily. I turn and look for him. There is no one there.

Once he came back though. Just once. He appeared beside me on the beach, grinning. That easy smile, the boyish slash of white in his brown face. 'That was close,' he said. I sighed with relief and we walked away.

What do I do with all this? I'm exhausted, flummoxed at how I'm going to make it through the day. I squirrel away the dream. I hate mornings: having to crawl out of the safety of my bed, having to face another day alone. Afternoons are better. The end of the day is in sight. I can relax and enjoy the evening light, enjoy the thought that soon the children will be fed and in bed. Though the afternoons are also when it can all fall apart. I have to guard against this. I have to plan activities, distractions; plan what is for dinner; plan my cheerfulness. If I'm not careful, if I forget or let the exhaustion sweep over me, let the blackness sit on my shoulder – if I don't force myself into activity – then my world slides towards chaos. These are the evenings I just get through. The kids have boiled eggs, cut-up carrot, cucumber and capsicum. I push aside the thought of a proper meal for them. Tell myself it could be worse – I could be filling them with crap from a fast-food shop (and probably would if there was one close by). Still, the guilt settles and I try not to look at how it could be. Try not to look at the table ready to receive a family. I tell myself that tomorrow it will be better; tomorrow I will make more effort; tomorrow I'll put some music on, pour myself a glass of wine, ask the kids to set the table, involve them while I prepare, meat, veges and dessert, and we will sit down like a family and pretend.

Usually the heaviness goes away when I pretend. Laughter lights the children's faces and I creep to the edge and peek out and see happiness. I know for a moment how lucky I am. It makes me brave and I shrug off the fear and embrace their delight in me. They think I'm wonderful because I put on some funky music and dance round the room. They think we're happy, and we are. I hope they can't see how hard-won that happiness is.

This morning when I woke, I took that dream of him with me as I sat on the veranda and watched the sun rise around the edge of the hills. I saw a sulphur-crested cockatoo high in the fir trees lining the drive. He looked at me, cocked his yellow crest, screeched his yellow rage at being disturbed and took off across the dawn sky. He took something with him, some seed of me, as he stole from the garden. I didn't understand it; I still don't. But my rage, my fear, my grief seeps to the surface in these early mornings and, if I sit quietly, something comes and takes a little of it away.

16

AFTER MY MOTHER DIED, we did the normal things. We saw a funeral director; we sat in inoffensive chairs and were shown the coffins; we talked of the service, my brother and I, so rational, sensible – our mother's children. Both of us put our emotions to one side and concentrated on the practicalities of the service: the flowers, speeches, church, supper, the particular wood of the coffin. All these things we effortlessly discussed. We shed no tears. We laughed lightly, mocking the choices we were faced with – should we go with the blond wood or the mahogany?

The woman on the other side of the desk asked us if we wanted a viewing. Ah yes, a viewing. Well, neither of us wanted one, but for others in the family it was important. The woman said, 'What would you like your mother dressed in?'

This was not a shock, a kind friend had warned me to bring some of my mother's clothes. I had chosen very carefully. They were clothes we had bought together. I knew so well what she would want. I brought her favourite lacy bra and matching underwear. I brought the soft, fine linen shirt we'd found in a little boutique in the city. I brought her favourite navy blue pants – elegant, tailored, showing off her petite figure. I brought her most comfortable shoes and also a beautiful scarf, one my brother had given her to hide the lump on the side of her neck.

I felt all was in order. I found myself explaining to the woman behind the desk the story of these clothes. Then I found myself asking, quite reasonably, I felt, for the clothes to be given back to me after they were finished with. I had thought this through. My mother would hate the waste of burning the clothes with her body. Why, I could wear them for years. My brother related this story later to the friends who had gathered on the veranda to support us with food and whisky, the tears streaming down his face and mine as we laughed, or was it cried, at the memory of the look of the woman behind the desk who, in all her years of organising funerals, had never been asked to return the clothes of a dead woman after she had no further use for them.

I remember my mother saying to an old friend that she felt she'd given her children everything they needed to make their way through life. Everything, that is, except the ability to cope with her death. I stood listening to her talking. As always, it irritated me that she'd made this – us – her life's work; had sacrificed herself so completely for her children. Yet in a way she was right about the death part. I had not prepared myself for her death. We hadn't even talked around it. It had just never come up before the cancer came. We didn't talk because it just happened. One day she was fine and the next she was going to die, and there was nothing anyone could do about it.

When we were small, my older brother had a fascination with running water. He would obsessively turn on every tap in the house so that they ran with startling ferocity. He would race from one room to another in wicked quietness while my mother was distracted, perhaps on the phone, or cooking dinner. The dripping of moisture down through the ceiling and onto the kitchen floor would often be the first sign they were running, or else someone would open the door into the sunken bathroom and step into ankle-deep water. Whichever way he was discovered, my brother's reaction was the same. He would place his hands over his ears and dance around in excitement, and then get very cross when the plug was pulled and the water gurgled away – though sometimes the sight of the water disappearing was enough to distract him from his tantrum and he would stand, captivated, by the sucking drain.

Hiding the plugs to the sinks, laundry tub and bath didn't stop him for long. He soon started to improvise and I often wondered if my mother wished she'd just left the sink plugs within easy reach after he learnt the effectiveness of flushing a whole roll of toilet paper down the toilet, and the thrill of watching the water rise to the top of the bowl, and the inevitable moment when the water slid over the edge, down the polished porcelain and onto the floor. What was it about, that moment my brother so loved? I think it was the rising tension, the race between the water spilling over the edge and being discovered. Perhaps the chaos was his way of resisting a world into which he didn't fit; his way of inverting the balance of power in the household. Though from my younger brother's and my own perspective, he seemed to have the power thing pretty well sewn up. Or perhaps it was simply what the experts called his 'autistic tendencies'. His twin obsessions were time and water – the one so quantifiable, the other so difficult to contain. Whatever the reasons for his compulsions, it made a lot of work for my mother.

Perhaps the first few times my brother blocked the toilet, my mother called a plumber. And she wasn't one to stay in the house and pay the plumber after the job was finished. Instead, I imagine her trekking down our long garden, watching him find the blockage, asking questions – how exactly did he work out where to put the electric eel that slithered its way through the mess? How did you test for blockages; how did you clear them most effectively? She must have foreseen the way my older brother was heading with the whole toilet thing. She had already coped with his discovery that a carton of washing powder tipped into a top-loading machine produced enough bubbles not only to fill our large laundry, but spill out into the hall and make its way inexorably towards the kitchen. Now the washing detergent was in the locked cupboard, along with the plugs. But this obsession with water was harder to control.

As my brother became more creative with what he would put down the toilet – basically anything that would flush – my mother became, out of necessity, an expert plumber. I imagine her saying to herself, 'It can't be that hard.' This was the thing about my mother, she let very few things defeat her. Whereas other middle-class suburban women might have been hospitalised with the stress of an autistic child, a husband with a public and demanding job that rendered him virtually invisible on the home front, and two other small children, my mother just knuckled down and got on with it.

My brother would flush underwear, socks, t-shirts, tea towels, hand towels, keys, soft toys – anything that would make it round the S bend – and eventually these items would catch against the tree roots, which fished for water through cracks in the ancient terracotta pipes. Then my mother would put on her oldest clothes, grab a shovel and trek down to the bottom of the garden to find where the pipe was blocked. And she would dig and scrape until she had cleared the pipe. This often involved her lying on the ground with her arm down the pipe, hauling out the stinking mess by hand.

Now I can't believe she did this. But it seemed so ordinary then, as if this was the kind of thing everyone's mother had to do. When she returned to the house, we would smell her before we saw her and it seemed normal that our mother would come inside stinking of shit, shower, get us dinner, tuck us into bed and then dress up to attend a work function with my father. She would walk out of the door, her hair piled high, smelling divine, but with the same set in her jaw as when she took on the blocked pipe.

When I think about what she left me with, it has to do with these two extremes. The woman who would kneel beside our beds in her ball gown and make up a story before she left for an official function was the same woman who was so ruthlessly independent – through fate, through circumstance, through personality – that she had become, without realising it, an effective plumber.

So is it any wonder that when she was first diagnosed with cancer, I continued to mark essays, give lectures and write research proposals? Cancer didn't stand a chance against her. I hadn't entertained the thought of her death, because in the face of her life it was too impossible to contemplate.

∞

From my desk I look out over the paddocks where she grew up. I think of the stories she used to tell me about her childhood in this place. About sneaking down to the shed with her sisters to watch the rams and ewes mating; of picking up the freshly baked bread from the letterbox where the baker dropped it off on his rounds, and eating the warm middle out of the loaf as she walked back up to the house on top of the hill; of having a bath from water warmed by a woodchip heater. They are simple stories, but my children love me to tell them. They are fascinated by the life she led in the same place they now call home. It's a rare sort of continuity: my children walk along the same track she used; they catch the bus along the same road on which she rode her pony to school; they sit in the same space she sat in to learn to read and write.

It feels safe to be a part of this continuity, but I also know my mother found this space claustrophobic. What is for me an escape was for her a vision of a future as a farmer's wife, which she didn't want to be a part of. But she loved this place and she's everywhere in it. So though we never talked of her death, and though I never contemplated losing her – simply because I needed her too much – and though her death was so fast, yet I buried her and said goodbye.

It was different between him and me. We'd talked about dying, though now I strain to hear the words we exchanged. We had a few of these talks, perhaps more deeply significant for him, as he'd already faced the possibility of dying. I wish I could recall more exactly what we spoke of in those moments. I wish I could hear back into those conversations. I can see the two of us walking, arms swinging together, an easy companionship through the night. There were clues I missed, for I hear them now in a silent beat of memory. But I was young and in love and oblivious to any darkness that might come between us, and my mother was a plumber and she'd taught me I could do anything.

17

IT'S NOW OVER A YEAR SINCE WE CAME OUT HERE and I realise I've lost my way back into my old life. I'm not sure that I can ever return to a city job. This Western District project is paying the bills and keeping me tenuously connected to my other life. It's writing and not teaching, which is great. But it's hard to apply the same sort of rigorous discipline as I had to at the university when I was combining the two. There's no library, no colleagues down the corridor to bounce ideas off. This emphasises my isolation. But the writing is also an escape. I can bury myself in the voices of another age because, really, I'm too scared to move. Any decision seems momentous. Often, just trying to work out whether to accept an invitation to dinner seems impossible. I waver, say yes, curse myself, say no, realise I should say yes – around it goes, all possibilities of certainty gone.

My feeling of inertia is made worse by the return of the drought. We'd waited for autumn rain. It didn't come. The ground is hard and the nights are now too long and cold for the grass to grow. Tension curls around my waiting, opens its mouth, hisses. Then, last night, it did rain. It fell as I bathed children, lit the fire and cooked dinner. Our house was a cocoon of warmth and light as outside raindrops lashed roofs and windows and fled into tanks. Beneath its tattoo I slept. Earlier in the afternoon the storm had gathered to the west. It had been circling all day, but the wind kept pushing it away. The air felt charged. I left the work on my desk and saddled Belle. We clattered down the drive. The wind pushed us along, whistling in my ears, lifting her tail and mane. Overhead, thunder rumbled and we rocketed across the paddock. Underneath my hands, I felt her muscles bunch and release, madness to be out in front of the storm, my voice lost in threads of wind.

Is this how he felt?

I ask this long after an answer is possible.

Is it this feeling of being on the edge of control, the edge of life, that made him seek the very big waves, the very dangerous reefs, the waterfalls, the rapids, the sheer mountainsides? My grief is bounded by such questions. They're the contour lines that map his shape more clearly than any explanation offered to me by medical staff of why he left. But it's the spaces in between the questions that are the unknown.

In Alaska, the maps we used to chart our hiking route were old army maps. Because the land is so huge, the lines on the map represented a larger area of elevation than on normal topographical maps. We might spend the evening poring over the map and planning our route for the next day, only to walk for a few hours and come to an invisible thirty-metre gorge, whose steep sides made a crossing difficult or sometimes impossible. If we couldn't get down and back up the gorge, we would have to walk perhaps hours out of our intended path to navigate these fissures in the earth.

That's what it feels like as I survey the landscape between my questions. Walking the lines of my grief, I keep tabs on the known, meticulously recording the day's activities to guard against the unknown trauma of tomorrow.

Tonight I sit on the couch and my muscles ache from riding. Miles Franklin wrote about this moment, which comes from having lived on the back of a horse. She knew the memory, the sensation of a horse moving her forwards, which grabs at you in the inbetween space of sleep and waking – always, for her, then. I know it too, and tonight when I crawl into bed I'll fall asleep to the urgent movement of the mare, the power of her stride as we raced the storm home. What if she'd bucked, or shied, propped and reared. Would I have sat on her with the easy confidence of my sixteen-year-old self; would I have delighted in her high spirits, joined her in being intoxicated by the electricity in the air? Or would I have found myself on the ground, mother of two, stiff, sore and dented? Of course, she didn't do any of those things and I take the exhilaration of the ride to bed, and fall asleep to drumming rain.

The rain is not enough. It's violent and heavy and washes away some of the dust. It fills the tanks for a moment, but really all it leaves in its trail is enough moisture to encourage a carpet of cat heads, which cripple the dogs and cause new lambs to stagger and fall. The cat heads have some strange component in them, because the stock become addicted to them and won't eat anything else, even if there is other feed in the paddock. The toxin causes the sheep to swell in the sun – their heads become misshapen, their ears blister and fall off. Those most severely affected must be locked up in the dark of the shed and fed hay until the poison leaches from their system.

I walk out into the night and the smell of the sheep camped out behind the house under the trees hits me like a slap to the face.

I held myself so tight at his funeral, I felt absurd. But the tears wouldn't come. Instead, I was swollen with our child, my breasts full and heavy. Fluid gathered in my body. Perhaps that was where all the tears were hiding – in my ankles and under my skin. Who wants to be that dramatic trope of the pregnant wife farewelling a husband who will never meet his child? I smiled and groped my way through the day. I kept bumping into things, hitting myself on objects that loomed out of the dark. I seemed to float some way above the crush of weeping people. Everywhere around me tears flowed, but for me there was no release; the tears stayed trapped beneath my skin, a poison that changed my shape.

∽

I had a dream about another man. I'm still so ensnared by my husband that I find it hard to believe my dreams are introducing me to someone new. 'Don't worry,' I whisper to him, 'it hasn't happened yet.'

In this dream I met a new man and straight away the connection between us was strong. He was dark, possibly

Italian, with curly hair. He was wildly rich and thought I was beautiful. Of course, I had this new body, and I felt long and slender. He seemed to have other girlfriends, but this didn't worry me unduly. We were in the city. Then we went to America, where he mostly lived. We went to his university and while we were there we wandered among his many girlfriends. Suddenly, as happens in dreams, there was an exam. I didn't have to take it but I did, and it seemed important to do well, even though I had never studied the subject. I wrote and wrote. The essay was partly concerning Australia, but I can't recall what I wrote, only that the ideas came to me fully formed and fast. All the other women wrote very little and seemed perplexed. My body was firm, my mind strong.

It was such a strange dream, to be loved by someone other than my husband. When as I think of it now, I can't recall feeling any love in return. It was comforting to imagine myself attracted to someone without sacrificing everything. I was not naïve, not young, not deceived by his wealth or good looks. But I still felt something, and though it wasn't love it was powerful. I scratch around the edges of the dream and all I can find is desire, and this in itself is strange because my husband is still seducing me, still appealing to me to let him back in.

Despite this dream, I can't let go. I go back over the day of the funeral again and I see I didn't really participate. Others farewelled him, made their peace, tried to understand, but I was a bystander. The crowd streamed past me. They took him with them, all their different versions of him. But I was left standing on the side because now he was dead I didn't know him anymore. I had no idea who it was I needed to say goodbye to.

What I want is some precise definition, something scientific that can be measured telling me who my husband had become and where the man I married went. Is this why I persist in seeing my grief as something that must be mapped? I want to see its outline, because perhaps, in its shadow, I will be able to see him again.

When I lost my mother, I knew her. Not everything, for everyone has secrets. But I knew the shape of her dying body. I could lie next to her and count the seconds and then the minutes between her breaths. When I cough in the night, the sound and the reverberation through my body evokes her. Ribbons of grief stream from my nose and mouth – I hold nothing back, I'm left desperate without her. It feels pure and powerful to mourn. Scary too. I lumber back to the edge of control. Find that once again morning comes, the day starts and the night is pushed back. But the growl in my chest remains. The imprint of her body never leaves me.

But him. I see him vanishing in front of me, always his back moving through the crowd. Is it because he shouldn't have died? Is it because he should have been safe? Or because he should be here with me now? Is this why I can't feel him on me anymore? For a long time after he left I felt a presence in the night. It wasn't the same as when I dreamt he was alive, but rather a feeling of being watched, of waking and having to convince myself there was no one in the room or the house but me and the kids. It wasn't comforting either, just spooky.

The night after he died I didn't turn off the light. I felt that if I succumbed to sleep maybe I'd be sucked away too. That's what it feels like when I think of him going. Words shadow me, such as sucked, pulled, hauled, wrenched, but mostly sucked, as though there was some sort of vacuum drawing him from me; something irresistible, powerful, which he couldn't fight, which kept drawing him to the edge of this life.

In those first nights after he really was gone, I knew that as soon as I let my mind sink into sleep, I would cease to hang on to this knowledge and would be pulled into that dark place near where I knew he was – underneath, down below into the heaviness and quiet. So I kept the light on, kept my sleep light, let my eyes close, but never embraced the dark or the peace.

It went on like this for weeks. Back then, the terror of his illness was much closer and it was a desperate time, during which I clawed my way through each day, only to face the night. But there is a part of me that now wants that closeness. It frightened me how scared I became of him, but now I look back and miss that rawness, miss even the shape of him, which was so unfamiliar yet was *something* between him and me.

I'm jealous that others have buried their version of him, but I'm left with an unfathomable emptiness, a gap I can't bridge.

This question of why one death is so different from another, one grief so perplexing, so hidden, and another so obvious, so instinctively harrowing, keeps niggling me. Saying good-bye to my mother was exquisitely painful. The more pain I felt, the more I knew how much I loved her and how much I would miss her. Why do I find an illness of the mind so much harder to understand? In theory, in relation to anyone else but him, I can rationalise, I can accept our minds get sick and we don't yet know how to heal them, that the instruments we use are clumsy. Is it simply the manner of his death that stops me seeing him? I fear it's more complicated than this: because he's lost to me, I can't follow any pattern of my grief.

18

I WONDER HOW MUCH OF OUR MEMORY is held in our heads and how much is in our blood, or muscle or bone. Put the sheep into a new paddock, a paddock they haven't been in for a long time, and they remember, collectively, where the water trough is. Take the horses down to their day paddocks in the morning and bring them back into the stable in the evening, and they will let you know that a piece of machinery has been moved from its normal place in the yard. These moments of remembering are all straightforward, but what I'm thinking about is the memory unconsciously within us. When you kill a rooster, its head, violently separate, is still. But its body resists death, flaps a protest. It would crow if it still had a mouth. Instead, it struts, twirls, staggers, falls. It fights and remembers life with every twitch, finds the ground, is drained of blood and only then gives in to death.

Is this me? Seeking the trace of him, the smell of life he may have left behind. My muscles ask no questions, they just hold his shape; hold it until he runs out like blood. My mind, meanwhile, seeks answers. Sometimes in other people's lives. I read and read. Squirrelled away from my professional life, I'm drawn to stories of others' secrets, and I don't seem to care whether these others are real or imagined. I'm searching for evidence that my life could have turned out differently, that my husband's death was not so inevitable.

Janet Frame seems an obvious place to start, and I read her late into the night. Outside, the air is heavy with cold, the dark silenced by frost. I read of her madness. My toes curl with the tension of her story, which exposes the inhumanity of the mental-health system. But in this quiet story there is hope – unlike my husband, Frame is rescued. Her genius lies in her acute observations, as if her years of being watched sharpened her faculties, so each instance in her day could be recalled and polished into something that made sense.

But her rescue challenges my carefully assembled façade. How could she be declared so far from sanity that the only conceivable solution to her state of mind was to perform a lobotomy? And yet this same mind was so brilliantly able to produce great works of literature. Her life further emphasises the tenuous grasp of reality we all must hold in order to continue to be judged sane.

In the midst of reading Frame, I organise another research trip to Melbourne, this time without the children. I fly down and stay in the middle of the city in a hotel within walking distance of the library. Frame's story has stirred up memories and, as I walk from my hotel along Little Collins Street, I search for distraction in the glitter of the window displays. I plan for a time when I might browse without sacrificing precious hours in the archive. Then I turn up Swanston Street and am swallowed by tourists; by the rancid smell of cheap takeaway food, even while my head is filled with clanging trams and the screech of brakes.

The library has a huge collection of manuscript material and the task of sifting through it to find the voices that most evocatively describe the experience of settlement is daunting. My walk brings me to the stairs of the library, a repository of intellectual endeavour, a bulkhead of sanity. Behind me, the traffic streams down Swanston Street, the trams rumble to a standstill and disgorge their loads of humanity. Movement, commerce, merchandise – more products call from windows to be bought. The door swings shut on the chaos of the street. I walk past the security guard, beneath the beautiful dome and climb the stairs to the sanctuary of the manuscript room.

So a thousand minutes after he's gone I stand at a threshold. Through the glass doors of the manuscript room, I can see the fishbowl of librarians who watch over the researchers reading precious documents. Somehow these librarians keep morphing into nurses. To ground myself I look up to the splendour of a book-lined room. But even here in another city, in this new life, a madman prowls his way around the boundaries. I watch him counting his steps. His street smell and street clothes mark him. I have to go back into the closed room where the archive is housed. So I raise my doctoral eyebrows, exercise my authority as a sane member of society, sign my name and am let into this world of documents. I step into the room, pick up a pencil, open the yellowed envelopes, focus on the closely written, faded script. I am not him. I will not be anything. But sane.

Back in the hotel, I pick up Primo Levi – his thesis on hope. To rid myself of the prowling madman, I copy a paragraph of Levi's careful prose into my journal. It has nothing to do with my research but I recognise in his words the impulse towards survival.

'It is lucky that it is not windy today. Strange, how in some way one always has the impression of being fortunate, how some chance happening, perhaps infinitesimal, stops us crossing the threshold of despair and allows us to live.'

Many mornings I have thought, 'It doesn't matter that it's 4.30 and the baby is awake and I have to get up, because I can make myself a cup of coffee and listen to the radio.' Many times I've said to myself that all I have to do is get through the next three hours and then the children will be in bed and hopefully asleep and I can lie on the couch and watch TV. It's awkward to place my small rewards, the complicated system I've developed to get through each day, next to Levi's ways of surviving a concentration camp, but the impulse is not so different. I recognise what he is doing. In the same way, I pluck out something so possible, so achievable, it pulls me into the future. It might be a program on the radio to listen to while getting dinner; it might be a chocolate and a cup of tea, and rarely is the length of time I must get through longer than a few hours. I run into trouble if I pin my hope to a moment too far away. I survive.

In Melbourne I eat out every night, work uninterrupted through the night and then sleep in the next morning. Back on the farm, I'm glad to be away from the city, but the enormity of my responsibilities falls heavily. There is wood to be split, a house to be kept tidy, dinners to be made, homework to be supervised, and under all these tasks is the fear I will not be able to keep doing all this.

Did he know how scared I'd be after he'd gone? How could he have done this to me? How could he leave me to face the world on my own? I constantly toss these questions up and they just echo back at me. My body seems to release memory after memory of his ability to calm me, and all the time my mind is shouting out at him to stay away, not to come close and hurt me all over again.

I walk out into the early morning cold. The stars haven't faded from the lightening sky. I can hear the roosters crowing their challenges, but I'm seeking comfort. In the stables the horses call to me softly. Belle gently places her nose to my face and blows her sweet breath over me. I halter her and walk over to Will, who sticks his big head through the bars of his stable and shoves me in the chest. We walk down the lane to a chorus of magpies and I slip off their halters and lean on the gate as the first weak rays of light peek from behind the hill. Will puts his head straight down to feed, but the mare moves briskly into a swinging trot and parades her beauty to the dawn sky.

Choosing to stay on out here feels like the riskiest thing I've ever done, but then in a moment my head and my heart meet and I can turn and walk in peace back up the lane to a waiting house with sleeping children and greet the day.

19

Because I prayed
this word:
I want

If Not, Winter: Fragments of Sappho, 22

THAT FIRST NIGHT AFTER HE LEFT, when I couldn't turn off the
light, I dreamt I was down in the sea, and only I could find
him beneath the rocks and reefs. I dreamt that, though they
searched, no one could find his body. They didn't want to call
me, but they had no choice because no one else knew where
to look for him. I'd found him so many times. I had a feeling
for it. An instinct. This time I dived down into the sea and
swam to him. He was deep, deep down, deeper than they had
thought to go. I swam to him and saw he was safe. He didn't
want to come up into the air again. So I came up. But I didn't

tell them where he was. I didn't say a word. I left him there under the sea and in my dream he was safe at last.

So, here's the thing I haven't said. Here's the thing I've circled and circled. I love him. I love him. I love him. Somehow in the mess that became us, I lost that knowledge. In all the anger and deceit at the things he had and hadn't done, I forgot how I loved. When it falls on me, I recoil as if hit by a striking snake. It hurts, shockingly. When I remember how I loved and how he loved, I am reduced to nothing. I just stop working. I sob as if there is no morning, as if this day has ended and there is no future. Out there under the night sky, I am alone with only the saltiness of tears to quench my desire.

I don't think this happens enough. Most of the time I am distracted by the children's needs. Did he think when he left it would be just me who mourned?

On the day he died, Lottie and I were staying on the farm. I'd left Sydney a few days earlier with her as he'd escaped once again from a hospital where he'd been taken after another suicide attempt. He'd turned up agitated and I'd given him an ultimatum that he must make a commitment to staying in hospital till his state stabilised. We said goodbye on that street corner. I told him I would wait for him to get himself sorted out, but that I had to go and look after myself. My body was not coping. I'd been having contractions months too early and my blood pressure was very high. The car was packed even as we stood under the light by the kerb. Next morning I drove away. The mountains became a wall behind us as we dropped down onto the plains.

I was told he was back in hospital. I was relieved, and being five hours from him allowed me to feel a little more in

134

control, as though now he couldn't drop from the sky and shake me with his state of mind.

A blue car came down the track. I was on the back of my uncle's ute with Lottie. We'd been out in the paddocks feeding sheep. It was a winter's day – cold earlier but now, morning-tea-time, perhaps, warm in the sun. I'd slept well. For a moment I let myself think my mother and brothers had just arrived to spend the weekend. But it was too early – they must have left before dawn.

But it couldn't have really happened.

He'd been saved so many times.

He'd never been serious.

It was always a cry for help.

So you see that couldn't be why they were here.

And then.

My mother got out of the car. She came towards me and her arms were around me, and I knew. And she had to be a mother and so did I.

There is little room for a mother's grief.

We sat on a step at the veranda's edge, my daughter and I. He was gone. He'd left me to do this. I want to hold him accountable. I want him to know what he did to her and what he did to me. He changed us. We sat there and I had to tell her. She cried and cried. She loved him without any question, without any demand, without any doubt in her eyes. There was no room for me to cry. No room for her even to crawl into my lap. She wanted to be small, to fit like a baby into my body. But there was another baby coming and right then I wondered how there would ever be enough room for both of them in me.

When my mother died, I didn't have to explain. I just took my children to the room where she was. I took her grand-daughter and she crawled onto the bed and lay beside my mother; I lay there too. I didn't have to be quite so brave, I didn't have to be quite so strong.

But when he left me, there was no choice. Everything in my body stayed standing. My bone structure held me up. I found that, somehow, I could still walk. I could still talk. I could feel the warm sun on my face, the chill of the air on my skin. I still moved through the day, but my body and mind had disconnected. My arms wrapped my daughter up and held her. My body sheltered the tiny baby within me. My mind stalled.

I lost my husband and also I lost the chance to mourn him sweetly and cleanly. There is no purity in my feelings for him. It takes such a lot of effort to climb through the memories of his illness. The procession of doctors and hospitals, crisis points located in time – my mother's birthday, when he pulled a knife on himself; my brother's birthday, when he escaped from hospital and arrived at the restaurant looking crazy; driving through the city searching for him as I tracked his ATM withdrawals over the phone.

To get away from those images, I have to swim down to a very great depth, where all the oxygen is sucked from the space around me. I need to find a place where the world is muffled and distorted. When I finally get there, which is not always, the grief is gashingly intense. I think of the women who slice their breasts with sharpened stones when they lose their husbands. They mark their bodies with a scar so people can see they're different – separate from other women, other wives, other mothers. When I get into that place, that sea cave of grief, I settle myself and lift to my eyes the treasures he left me, and I know that I too am marked.

20

LOOKING OUT OVER THE PADDOCKS tinged with a desperate green, not the riotous, violent growth of last year's spring, I realise that although the days are slowly lengthening and the soil is warming up, there has been no rain. Last year, the rain came and came. The grass grew in great swathes. It was so high we lost stock in paddocks that had previously been bare dirt. Tractors buzzed, hay was cut and put away for the next bad season. The crops grew. People bought new cars, new tractors; they stocked their paddocks to overflowing. Cattle brought higher and higher prices, everyone had grass. All around was a confidence that couldn't be pricked.

Twelve months on, the season's change has been swift and savage. This year there has been no winter rain, no spring rain. The crops are inches high when they should be a sea of green. The landscape is taking on the pinched look of January. What feed there is has dried off already.

Summer is a while off, but already I know it's going to be long. Even the land seems to warn against praying Sappho's words.

When my grandmother died, she left my mother an embroidery of the prunus tree she had sewn. It hangs on my wall. On the back my grandmother wrote, '4 Seasons of the Prunus Elvins at Marylebone'. It's a simple design of one tree in four garbs, made interesting by the way she used texture and colour. She chose spring as the starting point and the tree is covered in the most flamboyantly pink blossom, while the background is a deep emerald. The next is in summer and the tree is dressed in greens, light and dark, the background muted. My favourite is the winter tree. Its bare brown branches are stark on frosted wool. The autumn tree, covered in red, purple and pink leaves against a deep green, is highlighted with scattered leaves.

I like to look out of the window and match the tree with its mirror image on my wall. Now, as the evenings are lengthening, the blossom has bravely, stupidly, burst forth. In the paddocks, the canola crop is trying, despite the lack of rain, to turn the world gold. I hanker in the warmth of the sun and continue to read *If Not, Winter: Fragments of Sappho*. I'm not convinced by the sun's warmth – after all, it's only late August and, though my view is framed by blossom and bulbs pushing themselves from the earth and birds trailing prized twigs and drifts of wool to line their nests, I want to warn them all that winter is not finished yet. But, even as the world is seduced by the promises of spring, I find myself having to resist the temptation of feeling spoken to by these ancient words. I've been dipping in and out of the book for months, willing it to put meaning on the blankness of my grief – 'But me you have forgotten.'

I want to resurrect him piece by painful piece. I want to say goodbye to his body, because I never got to say it to him. I'm not alone in this. How many women have searched for the pieces of their lovers after battles, real and metaphorical? I think of Set, the god of the Underworld, who kills Osiris by cutting him into twelve pieces and scattering them into the mighty Nile. Set does not count on the determination, the redeeming passion, of Osiris's wife, Isis. She becomes my talisman, for she will not give in to death. She searches for each piece of Osiris and binds his body back together. I see her crawling through the mud and reeds, finding the reeking pieces of flesh, rescuing her love from the nibbles of tiny fish, crabs who fight over hacked flesh, the snapping jaws of crocodiles. But she loses too, for though she resurrects him and takes him to Anubis to be restored to life, her wish is impossible and she is still faced with seeing Osiris live in the shadow world of the dead.

∞

When my mother was dying, I sat beside her and watched how terrible life had become. Despite this, I saw her fight to hold on to it, and I also saw, though I did not want to, how hard dying could be.

In consultation with our family doctor, my brother and I decided to move our mother from the big city hospital into a small hospice by the sea. It was a relief to get her away from the teams of physiotherapists, dietitians and occupational therapists who poked and prodded, took blood, and forced movement then food upon a woman who craved only sleep.

In the new hospice we could all rest. We stopped having to fight the doctors; we stopped having to explain our decision to discontinue treatment to each new staff member who walked through the door. We allowed ourselves to stand still until it was all over.

Each afternoon, a cooling nor'easter would sweep the sea across the room. Each afternoon I'd come on my own and sit while a friend minded my kids. It was the week before Christmas. It was Christmas. It was New Year. It was school holidays and January on the coast. It was all those times, remorselessly, as my mother fought her way to the edge of death. The cancer that had first made itself real in the lump on her neck gradually claimed her whole body. By force of will she lived on. Even deep in a coma she wouldn't let go. She would rally when we walked into the room. Though she could give no sign of having seen us, her breathing would strengthen and regain its rhythm. No thing, nothing, had prepared me. Her breathing is etched into my body. I carry its rhyme, its strange, halting, desperate cadence. The hiccup of it, the body's reflex, the power of the mind to hold off death itself.

Death was going to have to be more stealthy, bide its time, wait for the coma to be deeper, wait for the messages to be whispered even more softly. Death was not to win her easily.

Even those last weeks of her life took on some bizarre routine. In the early evening I would leave the hospital and hurry home to have dinner with the kids, bathe them, read them stories and put them to bed. I had a friend who could withstand the ferocity of Charlie's two-year-old tantrums, who would wait for me with dinner and a glass of wine ready. She cooked, cleaned and looked after the kids through the horrendous final days.

On my way home to the haven she had created, I would drive past fat older women walking along the footpath by the sea, enjoying the cool evening breeze. And I wanted to spit at them. I wanted to wind down the window and scream abuse. They were so far from death and yet they hobbled on feeble legs, their shoulders rounded by the pull of their pendulous breasts, their strides short, their fat stomachs straining against too-tight clothes. Why did my mother lie paralysed in a hospital bed and have to fight for each breath, when only months before she'd risen early to run when the sea mist hung over the ocean?

After dinner I would go back to hospital to count the seconds between her breaths and then pass back into the early dawn to face another day when she would live, and we would live waiting for her to die. We told her again of the plans for our older brother. We told how we would cope; we whispered of the housing we had arranged, the around-the-clock care; we told her we had everything under control. She knew we were trying, but she also knew we were lying. For how could something that had never been more than adequate in the thirty-four years of my brother's life be suddenly all right now without her, without the one person who had guarded him from the world?

I think of my mother as I watch a ewe charge five dogs – all heat and bark and slashing teeth as they threaten her lambs.

The ewe's quietly maddened eyes stare down these attackers till their tails droop and they cease to circle. It's this instinct, this beating desperation, which held my mother. My mother had schooled herself over the last three decades of her life to always and through everything defend her helpless child. She fought a battle to the edge of herself and then fought some more, and it was terrible to watch.

But out of all this, at least I got to say goodbye to her. At least, when her death came, I had seen the persistence, the vast array of weapons it had at its disposal. I'd seen my mother slowly worn down. Even before she died, my grief seemed familiar and it was somehow comforting to let myself go in an emotion I'd subconsciously anticipated all my life. The shape of it makes it easier to wear. It swoops on me often, but mostly in places where I expect it. Mostly I know it so well that the sadness and the loneliness pass through me. I live it but, ultimately, I can move out from beneath it.

And what moves me from beneath is beauty – the way my mother taught me to see the world. This morning as I made the school lunches, I looked out of the window and caught the dawn flight of the peacock, like some prehistoric firebird: exotic and out of place, he swooped from his roost in the tall gum tree outside my kitchen, his tail a kaleidoscope, his flight carving a path through air as tight as sea.

Beauty also eventually lifts me from scrabbling beneath the waters in search of pieces of him. When I see beauty, I gasp, and in my gasping I'm forced to breathe. Life fills me and I'm somehow stitched together.

After the kids get onto the bus, I make myself a coffee and take it to the little east-facing veranda, where I sit in the late winter sunshine. Sappho's fragments lies open on top of my pile of 'must read' books. Sappho wins easily and I flip through the pages again.

'I want', and the want springs at me.

21

FOUR YEARS AFTER CHARLIE'S BIRTH, my mother's death, after saying goodbye to him under the light – it's only now as the summer comes on, as the drought tightens, I finally give in to tears, and then find them impossible to staunch. I'm no longer easily comforted. I'm no longer caught in the whirl of imagining juggling his illness and a newborn baby. Instead, I'm thrown back into the memories of our eleven years together. I can hear his laugh echo across the water as we paddle on the ocean. I can see him tossing our daughter high in the air above the waves and I look at our children and count, once again, what he and I have lost. I want to take that sharpened flintstone and cut myself from breast to breast. I want everyone to see the scars and know that however they imagine loss to be, it's bigger, harder, higher and deeper.

I'm left without even the dreams of him to accompany me. I don't know why they've stopped, or where they've gone, but now I have to conjure him from memory, he doesn't come when I'm unaware. While I was dreaming, my love and anger were both fuelled. Without them, without him, I'm empty, somehow made passive by his absence. I press my hands into my side; swamped by nausea I fight to stand and put dinner on the table.

It's surreal – I simply struggle to exist even so long after he died. Surely by now I'm looking for someone new, surely now I've got my life sewn back together. I should not be knocked by this heaviness. But I am. I most certainly am. He's a gunshot on a moonlit night, and my blood pulses out into the earth.

☙

Yesterday my son turned four and walked the corners of his earth waiting for his father to appear. For him the meaning of death is still not absolute. He has seen death on the farm – something is always dying or being born. Yet, he reasoned that such a momentous day as turning four would be as good a moment as any for his father to put in an appearance and lift him into the sky. His blue eyes looked at me and his small body clenched in excitement at the prospect of such flight. He was tense, ready for his father to materialise out of the hard dirt we stood on.

The calendar on the kitchen wall marks the marching days and I watch, detached, as anniversaries pass: birthdays, death days, ordinary days – all seem unlived. One of my ways of coping is to have the calendar full, especially on the days when I don't want to look at the date. But Charlie disarms me by his request. He's actually not fussy about which father appears – his whole concept of fathers is rather woozy, they are definitely something everyone else has – but his puzzled expression pulls me up and I wonder if I've been arrogant in thinking I can be both mother and father to my children.

Parts of me refuse to acknowledge time. How can four years have passed when I still struggle daily with his absence? The garbage mounts with frightening frequency and still I turn from it, hesitant – the job is not mine to perform. At least in Sydney all I had to do was drag the bins up the stairs and on to the street. Out here there is no garbage service, so I've been letting bottles and papers spill in the corners of the garage. The bins stink as I stamp another bag of rubbish into the top of them. I make an effort for a while – washing milk cartons, shrinking them up, rinsing tins and squashing them down – but inevitably life takes over, and eventually a trip to the tip cannot be avoided. On Sundays a progression of utes and trailers pass my front gate on the way there. I square my shoulders, load the car and join the blokes in the line-up.

I fight every definition of widowhood his death throws at me. I fight till I can fight no more and lie exhausted in the dust. He is the invisible adversary I shadow-box through the day. Every gathering I go to – every kids' birthday party, swimming carnival, trip to the beach, every ordinary moment – I have to push him away so I can see what I need to say, what I need to do. I wonder, as I walk away from a group of people, if they can see us jostling together. I wait for his response, his opinion, his insight. Do others see the pauses in my conversation? Do they hear the gaps he should fill?

There is a relentless cheeping as I write this. We have a two-day-old chicken in the house. You see, Lottie's chicken died. Sometime in the wee still hours of the morning, a fox found the gate open and went into the chook pen and stole her beloved. It was me, I left the gate open. When I woke, the only sign of Blinky was a trail of feathers down the garden. Lottie was going to be distraught. She'd saved that chicken from certain death at the beak of its surrogate mother. She heard my uncle say it wouldn't last longer than a few hours, so she brought it home and pleaded for its life on the lino floor of the kitchen. Passion soaked around the edges of her speech. We put the tiny bird in a shoebox under a lamp and fed it mashed boiled egg and soggy Weet-Bix until it was strong. And I didn't look after it, I didn't have to clean its box or feed it or change its water. She grew into a cuddly chook that could be picked up and carried round by small people; a chook who gloriously, miraculously, laid an egg. A chook who could be taken for rides on the back of a bike, taken down to cubby houses, smuggled into beds.

But the grief. The tears that wouldn't come for other sadnesses now spurted with artesian force. She asked me, where are these tears coming from, why do I have so many? And over and over she whispered that she would never see her again. This small person who has felt so much is once again placed on the rack. I want to guard her from the pain, but it keeps slapping her down. We talk about the chook. We talk about whether it is better to have had her, to have loved her and then be filled with this terrible pain when she dies, or whether to wish she'd never had the chook and therefore wouldn't have the pain. She considers this carefully.

We go and choose a new chicken from a friend up the road. She holds it to her heart all the way home and the tears stream down her cheeks.

If I had to describe my child's grief to you, I'd take a pencil and trace the shape of the tear in the fabric of herself. What you would see would not be a hole. It is not the empty space it once was, it would not have the shadow of an absence always leaning over her. I'm serious when I say it's the shape of a chook. It would also be the form of a pony. It would be an open sky above her; it would be rolling hills and dry creek beds. It would be the shape of here. Living away from the city has given her room to let her grief roll out. She has poured herself into the animals and into the land and sometimes she has lost and felt the pain again, but she is not so afraid.

It hasn't been easy convincing this child that life has a capacity for good. When her father died, she was not easily comforted with stories of reunions in heaven. But she did instinctively understand the absolute inviolability of death. She understood death had changed her.

I wanted to rescue her from that change. I wanted to rescue her from her serious self, from the small person who tried to shoulder my burden as well as her own. I want to give her the same stability I had growing up, and I hated the childhood she was living in the city – the routine of before-school care, school, after-school activities. This was made worse as my resources were stripped from me. Before my mother died, I could at least enliven this routine with afternoons when my daughter and my mother would cook, or write stories, or draw or dance or make up songs.

With my mother gone and without the balance of having

her father around to leaven my intensity, my daughter was slowly becoming more ethereal, less grounded, and before my eyes, far more fragile. Bedtime, always a struggle, became even more of a battlefield, as she hugged me tight, convincing herself that if she let me go I might disappear for good.

This same child who used to be afraid of the dark, of spiders, of being alone – who used to be afraid of everything – is now happy to play outside till nightfall; to lean into old tin feed bins so deep she has to hang from their edge, feet dangling to reach her pony's feed – she avoids the redback spiders lurking in the corners, but she doesn't shirk the task. It's as if I brought one child up to this world and the land has handed me back an infinitely stronger one.

Ever since we arrived, Lottie has been quietly campaigning for a milking cow. She has an ally in my uncle, who milked every morning for years and has only given it up in the last decade or so. The two of them compare notes on breeds, the merits of high milk production over cream content. My uncle tells stories of homemade butter and cheese and I remember the sweet taste of fresh, thick cream and the butter my aunt used to produce.

But cows are expensive. Lottie looks longingly at the Herefords solidly growing into steaks in the paddock, but they won't cut it as a milking cow. Then one morning my uncle pops his head in the door and asks Lottie if she's interested in buying a dairy calf. A neighbour up the road drives milk trucks and he's going back to Dubbo to pick up a calf for his family. For seventy bucks he can get her one too.

She flies to her room to check her financial situation and is back before my uncle and I can even exchange thoughts about the weather. She would love to buy a calf and here's the money.

The calves arrive a few days later. They are like big dogs and follow the kids up and down the stable. One is a week old and the other is three days old. I feel sad for their mothers. They are so sweet with their big brown eyes, their rough tongues and their shiny new hooves. The kids get their stall ready. It's like making a cubby, only more fun. They spread oaten hay in a deep pile and then make a nest for the babies to sleep in. My uncle whips up a clever feeder for their nuts and hay. The calves start off sucking milk through a teat attached to a wine bottle, but quickly learn how to slurp it out of a bucket.

Lottie has to choose which will be hers and which will go up the road in a few months' time. Everyone thinks she will choose the younger one, as one of its eyes and its coat are covered in very cute brown and white patches. But, after much consultation with various experts on dairy cows, she hardens her heart and chooses the plainer calf, because, as she explains to me seriously, 'Hetty' is the better type and she has a nicer temperament and temperament is important in a milking cow.

Lottie spends the winter getting up early so she can feed this calf. She goes to school with her jumper regularly spattered with milk. No one minds. Her teacher tells the class about all the funny things poddy calves get up to. Lottie writes a story about her calf.

Watching the calves one lunchtime, I have a rare moment of peace. I realise I'm watching a scene from my kids' childhood. Life out here is giving them new stories. The calves will become just one of their memories. My children will know what it feels like to be licked all over by the sandpaper tongue of a calf. How a kick from a tiny animal can strike faster than lightning. They're learning how to move softly, how to shift an animal much bigger than themselves by their body language. They carry the responsibility of a hungry animal depending on them to be fed, and they're learning the beauty of early mornings and late evenings, when jobs have to be done. Outside, they smell the sharp tang of the hay at the end of a hot day and they know how to put their hand under a chook and find the still-warm eggs. The two of them both know the weight of a dead lamb and the joy of a live one. These things are settling on the riverbed of their souls. They displace the sorrow and the silence with an earthy reality. The absence of their father and their grandmother will never leave them and will continue to shape the way they see the world. But I'm made peaceful knowing that bumping alongside these absences are calves and baby chickens.

I've been so careful to make sure the children are not defined by these deaths, but what, I wonder, is going to happen to me? I remember Dante's question at the beginning of *The Inferno*: 'What must we do in order to grow?'

I came out here to retreat, to hide, lick my wounds, to glint and glisten where no one could see me. I expected silence. I expected loneliness. I expected to inhabit that frontier landscape of hopelessness. But what I found was beauty and, Anne Carson tells me, existence depends on beauty. Yet, though calves asleep in the sun may soothe my soul, I'm beginning to question how much longer I will find comfort in my children building their new worlds. For without his presence in my dreams, I start scratching at the scab of loneliness. Perhaps I too have been expecting him to materialise out of this new earth.

Because, you see, I have this thing with him. This thing, which is so old between us, it mocks our mortal bodies and defies the drum of time. This thing comes in the night. This thing is familiar, it whispers ancient endearments in my ear, luring me from the present. This thing is dangerous. This thing is safety. This thing is white hot and burning cold.

This thing is desire.

Must this thing die too?

Last night I woke because there was a snake in my bed. I had turned over in my sleep and, as I turned, I sensed a presence. I opened my eyes. There was the snake, not curled beside me, not poised to attack, but working its way across my pillow. I leapt for the end of the bed and then stopped, terrified it would see my flight as an attack. I was unsure of how to get out of the bed without being bitten. I was frozen but my heart pumped against its cage and I was soaked in sweat. I inched my way from the bed, then panic took over and I scrambled for the floor. It was not until I was out of bed that my rational mind could convince every other part of me that it was distinctly unlikely there really was a snake in my bed. Only then could I sneak my hand towards the light, my senses prickled, not believing I was safe.

I have an instinct for snakes, though I'm never sure whether it's just low-level paranoia or something else. There is a spot down the lane where I've seen a huge snake, and sometimes when I walk past to get the horses, I know it's beside the track watching me. I've had snakes in the chook shed and in the garden, and we get some big ones up at the sheds and stables. They aren't harmless. They are deadly brown snakes, aggressive and quick to strike. My uncle is adept at killing them, though he'll leave them be if they are out in the paddocks. I'm not adept at killing them, though I'm determined to become so. But a snake in my bed! I head to the web for interpretations. The sites talk of transformation, of shedding old lives, of learning to live in new skins.

I finally ring a man who calls himself the 'PacMan'. He's in the local Yellow Pages under 'Rubbish'. For twenty-eight dollars a month he will take mine to the tip. It's a bargain.

22

WORDS ARE TWIRLING ROUND MY HEAD, but they are the wrong words. None of them has anything to do with early settlers facing flood, fire and famine in the Western District. These fragments of conversations I long to have keep getting in the way of the history I am meant to be writing. I can't get at what I want to say.

My impulse is to run. The place I want to be is empty – perhaps Wyoming . . . A new start, a fresh country – the unknown. But I'm trapped. I have a job to do, a book to write. If I run, I turn my children's world upside down, shaking them till everything they've put their trust in is gone.

I want to lie on the floor and not have to get up. I want to be responsible for only me. I want to be shaken and shaken again by all that has fallen out of my life. I turn from the computer and acknowledge that today no more words are going to be written. Instead, I try to think my way through the day, as it rushes in with its mundane demands. I tell myself to make a decision, any decision. But I can't even make a phone call for help. I drift to the garden, pick up a spade, instead, and dig.

I dig for my life. I cart wheelbarrows full of mulch from the hay shed, the chook shed, the shearing shed, the stable. Each trip feels like an adventure into my future. It feels defiant to plant things. Slowly, the garden is filling with cuttings given to me over a cup of tea – tiny offshoots of rosemary, lavendar and a dozen others I don't know the names for. I'm scared planting. I'm scared watering. I'm scared to make a home. Yet it's what I need and what the kids need. If I don't act defiantly, if I don't act with bravado, I will be swallowed alive.

Digging locates me, I stop struggling for words and concentrate on the ground. I push my spade into the soil and turn over the manure. The physical effort soothes and I start to try to tease out what it is I want from the future. I think perhaps if I can understand this, I'll be able to resist these attacks. But it shocks me to realise that I can answer this question for the kids but not for myself. The last few years have knocked all the wanting out of me. I realise I'm still too scared to pray those words alongside Sappho.

I think, 'I could've coped; I could've done it, if Mum hadn't died.' Maybe that's a lie, maybe I would have fallen apart anyway. But even if I had, at least there would have been someone around to pick up the pieces.

We need our mothers. Even when we're old, there's a place in all of us, a tender, delicate place that longs to be held, to be nurtured and protected. Even when our mothers have hurt us, shaped us in destructive ways, neglected us, left us, we still want them. The conversations I miss with my mother happen anyway. I almost know what she'll say, and it isn't the words I miss, or the advice, but the sound of her voice, the particular way she would look at me when I was speaking; the seriousness with which she took my day-to-day problems. The fact that I'd been woken six times by a sleep-resistant toddler; the dinner I spent an hour making, only for it to be turfed on the ground by a rebellious two-year-old; the number of times my daughter had vomited in the middle of the night. There are only so many people in the world who'll listen to these small things and feign interest.

I can still anticipate her advice, but I can't trust her voice in my head, because so often she would come at something from a radically different angle and transform my way of thinking and my view of her.

She was a witness to my life, to my childhood, my burgeoning identity, and all the myriad instances that make up who I've become. Now she is gone, I can't check with her how to make rock cakes, or lasagne, or ask her which cousin started talking first, or reading at the age of three. All this – the insignificant details of family – and so much beyond it is lost, and I feel a gaping blankness.

∞

After my husband died, after my baby was born and before my mother died, I visited a counsellor. She was recommended by one of the midwives at the hospital where I'd had Charlie. She was meant to be very good with children. I found her pleasant, simplistic and somewhat overwhelmed by my situation. The only piece of advice I remember her giving me was that I should somehow mark the day of our wedding anniversary with a small ceremony. Candles seemed clichéd, as did throwing flowers into the ocean. Nothing seemed fit to hold the heavy absence of him from this day.

Early on in our marriage, we had decided to splurge on a meal at a restaurant way out of our price range to celebrate our wedding anniversary. It quickly became a tradition, and I looked forward to those evenings as a time out of the ordinary. We talked of the year gone by and planned for the year to come. We invariably left satiated with food and wine, and with plans for our future.

So eventually I decided that to mark our anniversary I would continue this tradition. I booked a table for one, dressed up, left the kids with my mother and went out to dinner. I ordered champagne. I took a good book and my journal and I refused to feel sorry for myself. I read. I ordered wine. I ate. The lights winked from the harbour, the ferries steamed by. The room was full of couples. I wrote a letter to my husband reporting on my first six months without him. I told him I'd had our baby; Lottie had started school; I was negotiating my first book contract; I was about to go for an interview at Sydney University for a full-time job. I wrote into his absence, words pressing against the silence from the other side of the table.

Of course it was awkward to sit there without him, but he was still so real to me that his presence was palpable. I knew the comments he would have made, the food he would have chosen, and, if I'm honest, there was a small part of me that expected him to materialise and meet me in this place.

The letter I wrote is a strange combination of outrage at his absence and desperation at facing the future alone. It's all my strength and weakness entwined on the page. The words scramble on the precipice of my predicament; how to remember him – had he saved me from himself, had he made the ultimate sacrifice and freed me from the hideous rollercoaster of the last three months of his life – or had he taken everything precious, everything hopeful, every possibility of a future with him to the bottom of the sea? Of course, I know the answer to this question lies in neither the black nor the white. His position was too complicated, the future too unknown to predict what might have happened. Yet it's in between these two positions that I was caught.

I left the restaurant and caught a taxi home. My mother was waiting for me. She boiled the kettle. We sat at the bench and nursed our tea and talked about the evening. I told her what I'd had to eat and how I'd written to him and what it felt like to sit at a table alone. I told her how it made his absence more of a reality. Then Charlie woke and we sat on the couch and watched him feed and marvelled at his beauty.

I went the next year to another restaurant, and again my mother met me at the door with the kettle boiled and tea ready to be shared. The year after that she was dead. I didn't go to meet him again.

∽

Summer has arrived – forcefully. One day I lie drowsy in the early morning and realise I'm listening to the melting notes of the magpie as they slip into the air, a benediction on the dawn. Another day I pause from my work as a swarm of bees move like a furnace across the sky. In the background is the seductive cluck of the turtle dove calling his mate. The sounds of my outside world are sometimes broken by a vehicle rattling along the road, but as it fades, the birds and the bees and the busy ants close over the hole made by its passage. I'm learning to listen again. I'm raising the grille on my helmet and letting the cottonwool fall from my ears.

Yesterday it was 48 degrees. Today it's 16 degrees. We have just endured a two-week heatwave: the temperature has been above 45 every day and hasn't dropped below 30 at night. It's been so hot that leaving the house has felt like stepping into the blast of an industrial oven. The grass is straw, the gums are drooping and the paddocks outside my window are dressed in sombre summer colours of browns, washed-out yellows and muted greens. Even snakes would get sunburnt in such heat. We retreat inside, we can't even eat outside in the evening – at 8.30 it's still uncomfortably hot.

I'm reliant on my ancient air conditioner, which was put in about thirty years ago by my grandparents. Though it has been reconditioned since, you can still hear it thumping from as far away as the stables. I ration its use; we never leave it on at night; we turn it on only when we are in the house. And we pray it doesn't break down. It manages to lower the temperature of the two small rooms off the kitchen to a level that's liveable.

This heatwave feels different. Summer often brings a few days of 40-plus temperatures, but never weeks of it. After seven days, I wondered how much longer we can go on. All the old-timers reminisce of summers like this from their youth. They scoff at talk of global warming, or climate change, and reckon we've all gone soft. I notice strange things, for instance the country feels very clean, as if all the germs have been burnt off, scorched, in the radiant heat. I've taken to bringing the horses into the huge old stable – with its high roof and deep shade, it's open to the breezes but cool out of the sun. The two ponies and about ten of my uncle's pensioned-off old rams camp in there during the day. I bring the ponies up from their paddocks in the morning when everything is preparing for the heat to come, then put them out again in the evening so they can graze beneath the moon in the cool.

I've also spent the week trying to review a book. It's long overdue, but it's been too hot to sit in front of my computer so I've read instead.

When the cool change does come, it shocks us with its intensity. I woke this morning to find a cold southerly wind howling round the house and rain showers sweeping across the paddocks. The change has none of the relief of the electrical storm we usually get after such a heatwave. Instead, we are plunged into winter – the weather is foul, all gale-force winds and spitting rain.

I head up to the stable with the intention of filling the feeders with hay and leaving the ponies inside till the wind drops and the temperature rises. But when I get up there, they are desperate to be out in their paddocks. I tell them it's freezing out and they'll be much happier inside, where it's warm and dry. But, no, Lottie's little mare in particular is quite adamant she wants to go out. She parades up and down her stall, calls me when I look like returning to the house and she refuses to touch her hay. So I give in. I throw on their winter rugs, which is ludicrous when a day ago it was 45 degrees, and we walk down the lane to their paddocks. As soon as we step into the wind, I can see the mare thinking, 'Hang on, it's really cold out here.' I drop off old Will into his bare paddock and he looks at me with reproach, as if I'm nuts to have believed a flighty young thing like Belle – but I tell them they both asked to come out and I'm not bringing them back in for a few hours yet. Belle dances up the lane next to me, pulling gently on her lead, and I can feel her uncertainty play down the line. Laughing at her as we go into the paddock, I rub her neck and take off her head collar. Around us the wind swirls and, realising she's free, she stands on her hind legs and then bucks and corkscrews in a tight circle before galloping round the paddock. She makes the ground tremble with her searching stride and then she stops and bucks again. It's intoxicating to be encircled by so much power and beauty against the black storm clouds and pale, pale grass.

Walking back up the lane I'm startled to realise what a difference such a simple act as turning the horses out into the paddock makes. The mundane rush of getting the kids out of the door; the pressure of my writing deadline back at the house; and all the boring jobs that are waiting before I'll even sit in front of the computer – paying bills, washing, vacuuming, the lawn that needs mowing – burdens of living alone, seem to shrink in front of the beauty of a rearing horse. Being forced outside, being forced to look, has peeled the scales from my eyes and chipped away at the silence muffling my heart.

23

THE PHONE RINGS. It's the mother of one of my oldest friends. This woman is like a grandmother to my children. They treat her house like a second home, and happily stay the night there if I have to go away without them. Her house is a children's adventure playground, with wide concrete verandas, old trees and a garden filled with secret places. There is always something happening there. Outside the garden, ducks, chickens, poddy lambs, horses all poke their noses over the fence, while inside are a cat or two, and dogs – maybe a working pup, or a retiree from the dog yard near the stables.

But really it's the corgis that reign at her house. They patrol their kingdom with vim and vigour. They escort my friend's mother on her daily round of jobs – whether it's hanging out the washing, or shutting up the ducks and chooks, or a trip to the tip, the corgis are there, making the world go round. Monte is regal and allows himself to be admired and patted, once it's clear that you realise what an honour it is to stroke his golden coat. He's like a lion with a mantle of thick fur around his throat and the way he carries himself makes you forget his legs are only four inches long. Maude, his partner, can be a bit silly and forget herself when there is food around, but she is so happy about life in general that you forgive her these moments. She likes to play soccer with the kids, or lie on her back, short stumpy legs in the air, grinning in ecstasy at having her tummy scratched. The offspring of Maude and Monte are scattered around the countryside, but it's still a bit of a surprise to hear my friend's familiar voice on the other end of the phone asking if the kids could please have a corgi pup from Maude's latest litter for Christmas.

What can I say? I love these little dogs, but of all the dogs I've imagined owning, I've never contemplated a corgi. I've always imagined my next dog will be something big, something that makes an impression. A statement dog: a labrador perhaps, or a Rhodesian ridgeback, even a Staffordshire bull terrier – something that greets you with a loud bark at the gate. A corgi has never entered my head. Somehow the combination of their connection with royalty and their incongruous appearance – a large-dog body on very short legs – has secured for them a status in my head of dogs whom I admire, but enjoy from afar.

On the other hand, corgis are great dogs on a farm. They are happy to go places, but also happy to hang out in the garden. And the kids would be delirious with joy at a pup of their own. Daniel Dog is getting on and it would be good to have a young dog to buffer the loss of his departure when it finally comes. But a corgi, hilarious. I shake my head and say yes.

We spend the next few weeks visiting my friend even more frequently than normal so the kids can make their decision on which particular bundle of golden fluff will be theirs to take home. Finally a pup is chosen. He is just delicious, like a small golden wombat. I can't resist him and he quickly establishes himself as part of the household, though – I am firm – he is not to be an inside dog. With his thick coat, he is the perfect outside dog for our harsh winters and there is no way he is going to get a taste of what it's like to live a soft indoors life. I worry about how Daniel Dog will cope with a new arrival, but he just ignores the corgi, pretends he's not there, and when the puppy occasionally crosses his path, in that desperate, ingratiating way pups do when they see an older dog, he snarls in surprise and snaps at him.

We call the puppy Marmaduke and he becomes Duke for short – hardly original, but everyone is happy. My uncle has a young sheepdog pup just a bit older than Duke and the two of them rumble around the farmyard. But Duke is not like a Jack Russell pup or a kelpie: he is all fear and caution where they are bumptious and full of courage. He doesn't destroy very much outside my back door. He is wisely aware that horses might tread on him, cars and utes run him over, ewes bowl him down and cows trample him.

My uncle is accompanied everywhere by his pack of dogs. They herald his arrival and departure, but Duke doesn't want to be part of it. He quickly works into my routine and waits in the morning by the back door. Daniel Dog is getting too old to come with me on my morning jobs, but for Duke it's the very breath of life.

It's so much easier to get out of bed when I know there is a smiling corgi pup to greet me. Before the kids get up, I take the chook bucket from beneath the kitchen sink, add the delicacy of freshly caught mouse from the trap, let the back door slam behind me and trek up to the sheds. Duke bounces ahead of me – it doesn't matter what the weather is doing, he is happy to see me, happy to be out in the fresh morning. The ducks quack a great greeting as soon as they hear the door slam. I throw the scraps into their pen and watch them squabble with the chooks. Duke rushes up the line of dogs tied to their log kennels, touching noses with the young ones and wagging his tail, all cowering submission, to the older ones.

There is a great commotion of chooks, ducks and dogs – the day is on. Belle pokes her head from her stable and blows me a greeting. Part of my morning thrill is seeing her delicate head with its white star sticking out through the window. She can't help but twirl and spin on her hind legs at the noise the dogs are making. It insults her sensibilities. Every line of her shows her breeding and she is full of barely contained energy in the morning.

Duke and I walk into the stable and old Will also calls to us. He is as earthbound as she is the air. He has no breeding, no grace to his form, and yet I could sell him many times over simply for his faultless temperament. Duke sniffs around, searching for mice, for the trace of a bone, for all the interesting smells the night has left behind. I open Belle's stall and she touches me lightly with her nose, shifting her feet in the bedding of the stall. She's restless and it's only her manners that keep her still. I halter her and take off her night rugs. I can feel her skin crawl with impatience and she waves a leg at me in an effort to make me hurry.

When we first got her, I was worried by her antics in the stable. She was so touchy and temperamental. I'd see her buck and twirl in her stall, snort and cavort, and think, how on earth is my small daughter going to ride this thing? But when she is saddled and bridled, she is all good manners and, mostly, contained obedience. This morning she snorts in annoyance at the chooks scratching through the manure in her stall.

I'm finally ready and she walks out sedately. Next, we go and halter Will. He bumps me with his nose, sticks his head in the halter and marches out the gate. Duke trips on ahead, his tail like a flag, while chooks and ducks spread in a great cascade. As he's grown he looks more and more like a fox – a small solid fox, to be sure, but he has the same lovely deep red coat. We walk down the lane as the morning comes to life.

After I put the horses in their paddocks, I sit for a moment with my back against a fence post and watch the sun push its way across the paddocks. Mount Canobolas rises steeply behind the folding hills, and down below me the cattle are spread peacefully, feeding their way across the flat. Just for the moment the morning is mine – well, mine, a corgi companion's and two peacefully grazing ponies'.

24

MY UNCLE AND AUNT HAVE GONE AWAY for a week's break in the mountains. I'm in charge. My uncle has made it as easy as possible: all I really have to do is check the water every day, cast an inexpert eye over the stock and chuck them a bit of hay, give the dogs a run and water the garden. My biggest problem will be if the pump breaks down, and even if this happens, I can simply get on the phone and call in some expert neighbourly help. So it's not really a huge responsibility. Still, when they drive off, I feel a little alone.

I soon shrug this off and get into the swing of things. After the first couple of days, I find myself relishing my new role as manager. I set about my tasks with a new energy. The kids and I easily manage to feed up a ute-load of hay to the main mob of ewes. I slowly circle the paddock while Lottie and Charlie stand on the back and push the hay into the sea of sheep that swell up against the side of the ute and ebb away as the hay falls to earth.

I find a leak in a pipe and temporarily mend it – this

involves a lot of trekking back and forth to the machinery shed and puzzling over where everything is.

Early each morning I walk the dogs up the hill to the main house and turn on the water for the veges. Then I head out the back to water the trees. There are three working dogs: the eldest is an old huntaway – he's boss dog and everyone falls into line under him. Then there is a three-quarter kelpie/huntaway, who is sleek and light like a kelpie with the height and strength of the huntaway. The youngest is a black and tan kelpie, who is beautiful in his perfectly proportioned athlete's body. His glossy coat and tan eyebrows give him a rakish, movie-star glamour that the other two don't possess, but he's a bit useless compared to their no-glitz, just-get-the-job done attitude. Two Jack Russells complete my uncle's staff, both of whom are wonderful hunters and great characters, but complete nuisances when it comes to getting any sort of stock work done. Still, they like to be involved and their own inflated sense of self-importance means they can't bear to see anyone attempt a bit of work without their help. I add the new corgi pup to the line-up, while Daniel Dog graces us with his presence to bring up the rear.

We walk across the flat and up through the homestead paddock. It's a fresh morning; I can feel the heat shimmering in the sun's rays, but the air is still too cool for it to have any sting. My uncle has left the rams in the homestead paddock so I can easily keep an eye on them. I wander in a bit of a dream up the hill as the dogs dart around my feet, following interesting scents then coming back to check on my progress. Daniel Dog and old Mac, the chief work dog, walk sedately behind me. Occasionally they raise a lip and show their incisor teeth if one of the young dogs bounces too enthusiastically up to them.

I look round for the rams, who should still be feeding at this time of the morning, but I can't see them anywhere. I extend our walk – they must be over the hill, tucked down in the gully already camped for the heat of the day. We trek to the top and look down. I'm getting hot. No rams there. Bugger. Where could they be? I ask the staff to see if they can find them and they head off in various directions, only to return in less than a minute, their raised eyebrows and pricked ears clearly telling me that they can't find them either. Hmm.

I head up to the garden and do the watering, then we go home the long way down the back of the hill and up the end of the flat, in case they're in the far corner of the paddock. But no, the paddock is empty of rams, though yesterday there were definitely sixty in here. I walk back to the sheds and tie up the corgi, the young kelpie and both Jack Russells, then hop in the old farm ute. The two old working dogs are on the back in an instant, tails wagging and mouths grinning at this first sign of real action in over three days. They're bored and keen to work. Those left behind immediately start howling at the injustice of it, but I harden my heart. The last thing I need when I find these rams is four more dogs 'helping'.

I make an exception for Daniel Dog, though, and he jumps neatly into the cabin for moral support. We drive off up the track. I tell the dogs to keep a look out for the rams and I can see them scanning each paddock as we head slowly up the hill. My heart is sinking because now I know where these rams have gone – straight up to the ewes. They've

173

obviously pushed through the first set of gates and have been lucky enough to find their way unimpeded to all the ladies in the top paddock. I find myself silently praying that the fence has stopped them. If it hasn't, I'll have to bring the whole lot down and draft them off in the yards, and for that I'll need help.

We chug our way to the last paddock of ewes and there, thank God, are sixty rams lined up on the right side of the fence. I stop the ute. The dogs look at me, awaiting orders. I unclip the younger dog and, mustering my most authorative voice, tell both of them to 'go back', at the same time as waving my arm in the vague direction of the sheep in what I hope is the appropriate manner. Both dogs streak off and before I've even had time to congratulate myself on this early success, all the rams, tightly bunched, are milling in front of me with two dogs awaiting more instructions.

This next bit gets tricky. There are two ways of working dogs – some people teach them to work the stock towards them and others teach them to push the stock away. At this point I'm blowed if I can remember which position my uncle takes. I look at the dogs and say in beseeching tones, 'We've got to put them back where they were.'

The dogs are a little unclear on this complex sentence and continue to hold the sheep in front me, waiting for a more direct instruction. I try pointing towards the gate and Mac cocks an ear at me – I can see him thinking he's going to have to take control soon, as I'm proving hopeless. I try another couple of voice commands and a bit more body language and suddenly Mac understands what I want and he has the mob moving down the hill.

I'm so relieved and triumphant. I hop into the ute and trundle along behind the dogs, shutting the gates as I go. Daniel Dog puts his front feet on the dash and reinforces my instructions by barking at the other dogs as we steam down the hill. The rams are cross – they don't want to go back to their old paddock. But after a couple of their escape attempts are thwarted by my new best friends, they settle into a steady plod. At each new paddock Mac looks back to check if we are to keep going. I make encouraging noises – we keep going.

When we finally get back to the homestead paddock, I don't even have to whistle the dogs onto the ute – they are up on the back before I've even communicated that the job is over. I resist hugging them, but I'm so grateful that they worked for me – they could have just nicked off (which I'm sure they would have if my uncle had been around) and left me stranded.

We head off to the sheds, where we are greeted with great delight by those left behind. I park the ute, feed the dogs, tie them up and head back to the house just as it's starting to get really hot. The kids are up and pottering around getting breakfast. I sink into a chair on the porch and take my boots off. Daniel Dog and Duke flop in the shade. I tell the kids where I've been and explain how well the dogs worked for me. DD shoots me a look as if to say that the whole thing would have been a disaster if he hadn't been supervising. After making this point, he growls at the corgi, who is forgetting himself and trying to make friends, puts his head on his paws and clocks off for the day.

His superiority makes me laugh and I feel lightly flushed with success and independence. The heat is brewing for a scorcher, but I can't heed its warning and suddenly I feel unexpectedly hopeful. Sappho's words, 'I want,' spring unbidden into my head and I feel branded when I utter, 'I want this.' Dogs asleep on the lawn, kids happily pottering. Is it safety, or something more?

25

THIS MORNING MY UNCLE DUCKED HIS HEAD round the stable as I was putting the ponies out and asked if the kids wanted to give him a hand moving the heifers and bull down to the creek flats. I said I wasn't sure how much 'help' they'd be but I was sure they'd love to go for the ride.

We saddled up and headed to the paddocks. Lottie rode her mare and Charlie poked along behind on old Will, his grass rein firmly tied up. The kids circled the paddock scanning for a flash of red and white, or the black of the bull. Eventually they found them. Lottie's mare is not used to stock work and she is certainly not used to being asked to plough through a paddock of nearly waist-high saffron thistles. She tried to jump them but only managed to land in another patch, which she kicked at, leaping sideways. She couldn't escape them, and my heart was in my mouth as I watched her rear and carry on. But Lottie just laughed at her and urged her after the heifers in what looked like a series of kangaroo bounds and cat leaps. Will, God bless him, ploughed through the middle of the thistles, knowing full well if he attempted a leap his small rider would end up on the ground.

Lottie got the heifers moving and they thundered past Charlie. For a moment I thought Will was going to spring into action and turn them, and I could see him thinking about it because he knew what to do. Fortunately he decided better of it and trotted sedately after them. Lottie went flashing by him and turned them down the fence line, and after a while the young cows settled and dropped back to trot along with the bull.

Duke came along for the run and he was no trouble – if he was a Jack Russell he'd be trouble. When the action hotted up and everyone started yelling and waving their hands, he made himself scarce, while my uncle's Jack Russells were in the thick of it. They got in the way, nearly got kicked by a heifer, trampled by the bull and were in exactly the wrong place to get the herd through the gate. They got yelled at, stones thrown at them and still they thought the job couldn't be done without them. Duke slunk behind the ute and waited for everything to quieten down. When it did, he came back again to trot behind Will's heels.

The kids tailed the cattle down to the creek. I could hear Charlie singing as he rode along. He wasn't really concentrating on the job, and truth be told he'd much prefer to be riding a motorbike. But he was happy, and being up on the back of Will gave him a feeling of conquest and mobility. I thought of all the other things I could be doing in the school holidays and none of them came close to watching my kids push some cattle along a dusty paddock.

~

Our life is unfurling out here and I've become aware of a new absence, that my husband is no longer taking up the same sort of space in my head. The feeling is the same as when you walk, leaning into a big wind, and then round a corner nearly fall over because the wind, the thing that was both holding you up and holding you back, has gone.

I'm not sure why I haven't moved on to someone else – of course, the most obvious answer is because there is no one else around. Although the practical side of me argues this persuasively, I think it's perhaps more complicated than a simple lack of opportunity. I look at other women who've lost partners through death or divorce and see how quickly they pick up a new relationship. I know I couldn't do this, but I also look at women who haven't found anyone else and I don't want to be caught in the past, sucked dry by the love of a ghost who can't touch me.

My girlfriend tells me that once she dreams about having sex with a man she has met, she nearly always ends up sleeping with him. If she doesn't dream it, it doesn't happen.

So far, my dreams are of men I haven't met, men made of pieces of blue. In one dream I am out in an empty landscape, a place where the sky meets the land in a great amphitheatre rimmed with trees. I come upon a shed. There's nothing around it – nothing. I've driven and driven to get there. I walk into the shed and there's a man. He's waiting for me, but he's acutely out of place. He's beautiful, powerful in a way, but I'm worried about his survival in this alien landscape. I think, well, I'm all right, I know the way out of here, I've got a vehicle and a nearly-full tank of fuel – but how is he going to survive once I leave? Then I shove all thoughts of

179

his wellbeing aside and we enjoy each other and I do walk out of the shed and get into my vehicle and drive away, and later, when I'm closer to being awake, I realise he wasn't a man at all, but a racing pigeon who'd been blown off course by the big storm I'd driven through. I often wonder about that pigeon and think how it had no chance to get home and that I would like to find my way back into the dream and rescue the bird.

26

'Speak not soothingly to me of death, oh glorious
Odysseus. I would choose so that I might live
on earth to be the servant of a penniless man than to
be lord over all the dead.'

Ghost of Achilles, Book II, *Odyssey*

QUITE SUDDENLY, IN THE WAY OLD DOGS DO, Daniel Dog
has deteriorated. He's gone from pottering through his
days, following the sun around the house, to being
uncomfortable in his gut. He's become distended and
swollen. He's obviously had a tumour growing inside him
for some time, but this week it seems to have doubled in
size. That it happens when, out of nowhere, I have a man in
the house is disconcerting. The man is staying up the road
while he has some work in the big goldmine nearby. He

only drops in for dinner, but still, he's very much here. At first, Daniel Dog circled the man warily, then he just heaved a sigh, gave in and ignored him.

I'm surprised to be attracted to anyone again; to have found something in me to respond to a man when previously there has been no wanting there. I read books about women deep in grief who simply desire the knowledge of another body. They write about seeking the moment of connection, as if sex somehow locates them back in their body; as if the physical contact, the skin on skin, the real presence of another body actively inhabiting their own displaces the pain of the absent one. I haven't had that desire. Perhaps it was Charlie's tiny baby needs that protected me – after all, though it's not sex, it is physical to feed a baby, hold a baby. Perhaps it was because my husband was such an active presence in my dreams, or perhaps I was just too busy with earning money, with staying sane.

But then this man walks around the corner and hits me in the guts. He doesn't have to say anything for me to know I'm in trouble. There's no other way of describing it. There is a current, a rippling. He returns the interest, or does he? Is there a connection? Is it him, or does he just coincide with my newly increased sense of visibility?

He comes to dinner and we sit on either side of the dining-room table. Highly polished wood measures the distance between us. He works me round the kitchen, getting in the way, placing his body across my path, standing behind me, looking over my shoulder. It makes me laugh and draws a spark from somewhere. He turns the meat on the barbecue and I enjoy the feeling of companionship; of having someone to talk to; of sitting on the back step and looking at a man. He sways into me as I pass carrying plates of food.

I've had no interest from any other men – well, that's not quite true. Shortly after I arrived up here, the local nurse rang me and asked me out motorbike riding with him. He arrived at pony club to talk to me, wrote me a letter with exquisitely fashioned penmanship and eventually, after I'd explained I was not interested in a dozen different ways, he left me alone. It can only be described as an embarrassing episode for us both. It also seemed to confirm to me my new status as an older mother with two small children. A woman that a man such as this nurse might think he had a chance with – a desperate woman willing to take on any man who fell across my path. That nurse was right. I was desperate. But not for a man.

But this man is different, and I'm different too.

∞

Daniel Dog is not going to survive. I watch him watching me, and feel studied. Finally the question goes from his eyes and I ring the vet in the morning and take him in. He's so deep in himself now that he falls asleep on the floor of the car and all I have to do when we arrive is lift him up and hold him on my lap as they inject the thin green drug into his vein. His little body relaxes and in that moment I appreciate how much pain he has been in.

Driving home, his absence strums against the muscles tight across my stomach. Can I survive without him? When he leaves, there is a hole again. I realise the carefully crafted solitude, the moments of beauty that I find in most days are changed.

The dog has had more luck than any Jack Russell I've ever heard of, and has been my companion through the darkest days. Why is he choosing this moment, this very moment, to leave me? The tears, which I always struggle to find, slide down my cheeks. I howl into the sanctuary of the car, because there is no one to staunch them, no one to kiss them away, no one for me to sink into, no one whom I will trust with the depth of this loss.

He's been with me for eighteen years, and – the echo – he's been with me for eleven years then – much fainter – he's been with me five minutes.

By the time night has fallen, I've dug a deep hole under the plum tree. I've lowered his body into it and covered him with stones and earth. I lean against the tree with an array of digging implements around me. I could have asked my uncle to help me, I could have waited for the man to arrive, but I don't want anyone to see me like this. I don't want them to know how much this small, senile dog meant to me. I don't want them to see the scars his death has revealed again. The grief makes me feel ugly, and I need a moment to put myself back together before I can face anyone.

So I go inside and stand under the shower for longer than our rainwater tank can really cope with. I wash my hair, I scrub my whole body and put on clean, fresh clothes. I slather cream all over me and hope the stench of death is covered. There is a light on the road, a creak of the door, the tinkle of the cowbell as it swings against the wood and I straighten my shoulders and greet this new thing that has dared to step into my world.

Later, long after he goes back to his other life, I walk across the road to watch Lottie work her mare down on the ram flat. Will grazes a circle around me – Charlie rode him for about ten minutes before losing interest and going off to play in the old ram shed. I lie down on the stiff grass. It's coated in dirt from the dust storms we've been having, and I know when I get up my jeans and top will be dirty, but I don't care. The light is long and all I can hear is the rhythmic chomping of Will as he grazes, and the even older rhythm of Belle pacing patterns in front of me. The mare glows bronze in the light and Lottie's face is a study of concentration as she gives her almost invisible aids for Belle to shorten or lengthen her stride, to canter, to change direction, to move sideways or halt.

I lie full length on the ground and watch the mare's tail swing from side to side as she trots out at Lottie's command. I can see the tremendous athleticism and the sometimes barely controlled energy, but tonight her tail swings like a banner and Lottie has a smile on her that touches the edges of me. Duke suddenly appears. He's been in the ram shed with Charlie and has come back to check I haven't moved. And I haven't moved. I don't want to move. I want to soak this up. I want to lie on the ground and be absolved. And what strikes me is that I am.

I'm different. It's so simple. But it has taken so long. I'm different. I lie here and feel the earth beneath my back and I realise this place is tattooed into me. I can get up and walk away from this moment and know there is another moment just the same waiting for me tomorrow. I watch our child riding her horse. She sits tall in the saddle, perfectly

185

balanced. She laughs and throws away the reins. This is the signal for the end of their session. The mare stretches her elegant neck and canters around the paddock. I can taste the freedom in it – the mare's stride swallows the earth and suddenly my small child is up out of the saddle. She's picked up the bridle and is urging the mare forwards, the drum of hooves echoing through the earth. Old Will spins and pricks his ears and the two of us watch the two of them circle the paddock at a gallop. They come to a thunderous halt in front of us and the mare sucks in the air in deep satisfied gasps. Her veins stand out and when I touch her she feels like warmed silk.

The peace of this moment now sits alongside a newly awakened sense of being alone. It's not distressing, but it's new. Since that man walked back out of the door, I've been sitting with a sense of displacement.

I'm happy. I can lie down on the grass and feel the world around and receive the peace it has to offer. But alongside this deepening sense of contentment is an itch. My husband has gone and an unattainable man has looked at me and something has changed.

Walking up the ram flat, I realise that 'I want'. I want to be held again. I want to feel someone's arms around me through the night. I want to be argued with, I want to be lifted from my feet by arms stronger than mine. I want to be loved and I want to be touched.

Then I laugh. I catch sight of my clothes line groaning under the weight of the weekly washing. Towels and sheets, footy and hockey uniforms, jodhpurs and assorted lacy smalls all dance gaily beneath the warm wind. The line is groaning because there are a couple of saddle cloths, a horse rug, not to mention school uniforms.

I leave Lottie to unsaddle, hose and brush her mare, then rug and feed her. The washing on the line waits for me. I go inside to fetch the laundry basket and I can hear the kids calling to the chooks and ducks to make sure they are all locked up for the night. Lottie treks over to the hayshed and loads a bale of hay onto the trolley to pull back to the stables. Duke dances along in front of her and I unpeg the washing. My longing for companionship suddenly seems ridiculous and, as I stand under the line and fold the washing, I ask myself what it would feel like to have to wash a man's enormous underwear, his dirty canvas pants, his heavily soiled work clothes. Do I ever want to do someone else's washing again?

I think, it would have to be quite a man.

27

I'VE COME TO A HOUSE ON THE COAST. I'm meant to be at an historical conference in Queensland. This is the first year I've been brave enough not to go. The conference has always been something to look forward to – a time away from the kids, catching up with friends and colleagues, mixing once again in the world of ideas. I've always told myself it's especially important to attend now I live so far away. But somehow at the last minute, after I'd organised the kids, accommodation, plane fares, I couldn't face it. Instead, I've rung old family friends and arranged to stay in their empty beach house for a week to write something that is not history.

Doing this marks a shift. I'm taking this new writing seriously; I'm stepping out of my life and retreating to work on something that sits right outside my university career. Yesterday I drove over the mountains, skirted along the edge of the city and hopped onto the conveyor belt that is the freeway. There, among all the tradies in their utes and light trucks, I was carried over the Hawkesbury bridge and onto the Central Coast. This area is so familiar. I've spent summers here since we were small children; I've lived here, looking out over the golden sweep of the beach, the monolith of the headland to the east and the line-up of tankers along the dark horizon at night. But this time I can't return to our little house on the cliff. My younger brother is living in it and it's too small to contain both our creative energies. Hence I've come to the new house.

This house is on a different cliff, it looks west and north – over the bay and the beach – and it's more protected from the wind. The view is wide, but you don't feel as though it belts you over the head from every direction as you do when you walk into our little house. So it's different – the same place but different.

It takes me a while to settle in. I've got three days of uninterrupted time and already the hours and minutes feel as though they're marked as staccato notes on my page. I know that if I concentrated on the sum, I could count exactly how much time is waiting to be filled with the tapping of my fingers. But the quiet, the lack of background noise – fighting kids, TV, dogs barking, balls being kicked in the garden – make the silence between the minutes stretch dauntingly ahead of me.

It's July but the temperature is mild, the air soft and I don't need the boots, scarves, coats, heavy jumpers or any of the other clothes I threw into my bag. I'm not sure where I'm going to work, but before long it becomes obvious that the only place is in front of the huge cathedral window that faces northeast and looks out over the beach. I drag a chair around and place myself in the centre of the view.

It's challenging to be here. Last night before I went to sleep in a strange bed, in a strange house, I had to remind myself that my husband was dead. Why does it suddenly feel as if he is going to tap on the window in the middle of the night? Is it the absence of Daniel Dog, who has always accompanied me on this sort of retreat? I haven't had to wrestle with this for a long time. But the coastal landscape seems to draw him up, conjure him from the sand and salt and water. These were his elements, the smell and taste of him. Salt on his skin, on my tongue. Still, his presence is not as strong as it was and, somewhat surprisingly, I go to sleep easily and I'm undisturbed by dreams.

Running in the morning, I find myself jostling with him for possession of this place. But I can feel my confidence returning and suddenly I don't like the feeling of being pushed out by his memory. I want to be part of a new thing; I no longer want to be constrained by memories, good or bad. I've been content to let him have the coast, it's not something I've had the energy to contest, but now I can feel myself stretching into something new and I want this place back again. I want to feel comfortable here. Anger fuels my stride and my breath comes jagged and raw. Whenever exhaustion threatens to slow me, I see him ahead of me and I grit my teeth and chase him down. I run myself to a standstill. My heart thumps against my chest, the blood sings in my ears, my muscles feel fat with lactic acid and tremble when I try to walk. Eventually my breath returns to normal and, when I'm capable of it, I have to laugh. I could never catch him when he was alive, why would I think I could now hunt down his ghost?

28

THERE ARE A LOT OF DIFFERENT THEORIES on snakes: they don't like freshly cut lawns; they won't cross a white line on the ground; if you have peacocks you won't have snakes. This last one I know is wrong because we've got peacocks and we've got snakes. The peacocks are quiet through winter. They drop their tail feathers at the end of summer and when they have no tail they don't draw attention to themselves, taking silent steps around the farmyard. But in the summer on a moonlit night, when their tails are a cascade of colour, they call and call. Their cry is harsh and echoes through the valley. The noise drives some people crazy, but I love it. I love half-waking in the dark to hear a peacock call to the world that a truck has just passed through the stillness of the night, or a fox has crept beneath his high perch, or a bull moans his longing through the midnight hour. All the would-be silent movements of the semi-dark are seen by these supreme nightwatchmen. I wonder as I lie sweating beneath my sheet, do they see the other world too?

For a long time, we've had two peacocks. We did have three, but in an unfortunate incident with an overexcited Jack Russell, the third peacock was killed. My uncle and I were devastated. The two remaining peacocks hang out together, but they are very territorial. One roosts on the electricity pole behind the stable. They are hardy birds because he's up there in the rain and heavy frosts and, most dramatically, in the high wind, when his tail becomes a sail and I've no idea how he holds on. The other peacock is the less dominant one and he roosts in the huge gum tree in the paddock beside my cottage. He's the one I watch swoop from his roost each morning, and he's the one who is tempted to sit on my car or admire himself in the bedroom windows by perching on the railing of the eastern porch.

My aunt is quite happy we only have two male peacocks. She hates them and encourages the dogs to chase them. She hates their harsh call and the mess they make. Me, I can't believe something so beautiful can be in front of me when I look out of the window, so I'm prepared to forgive them their vanity. Because, really, if you looked like that, wouldn't you find a reflective surface to admire yourself in at every chance?

When Lottie's mare first arrived, I was never sure which was more heart-stoppingly terrifying for her – the tractor always coming and going, pulling or pushing one piece of strange-looking farm machinery after another, or the peacocks, who would appear from around the corner of the stable pursued by a herd of dogs, only to sail over her head and perch in the window of her stable. The first time the mare saw one fan its tail, she acted as if the world had ended and all we could do was laugh at her terror. She eventually saw the funny side and, after a week or so, accepted their sudden appearances or calls without flicking an ear. Still, I think the mare is on my aunt's side in believing the world would be a calmer place without the peacock.

My uncle and I share a taste for the exotic in bird life and we often meet on our respective morning rounds and stand silenced for a moment by their shimmering display. We feel a bit sorry for the old boys because they only have the chooks to try to seduce with their fabulous dance. But this doesn't seem to discourage them and a dozen times a day I will walk past one of them hard at work to impress an indifferent hen. I wonder, why don't they take a leaf out of the playbooks of one of the many roosters who strut their stuff around the farmyard? For, though the roosters call their dominance to each other in loud acts of bravado, when it comes to seducing hens, they don't much go in for making a good impression – it's more of a quick sprint, followed by an even quicker act of consummation and then on with the rest of the day. But the peacocks don't dress in all their finery to indulge in such footy-boy tactics. Instead, they spend hours in the chook yard trying to impress their beauty on some hapless, cornered hen, who goes on pecking at what lies on the ground, indifferent to the splendour before her.

My uncle and I agree that what we really need is a peahen. We don't do anything about this for a long time. Then, in the way of these things, a neighbour up the road has a pen full of roosters she wants to get rid of, and two peahens. My uncle will take the roosters and suggests we swap one of our peacocks for one of her peahens.

The deal is done and all we have to do is catch a peacock. This is trickier than it sounds, especially because my uncle specifically wants to get rid of the peacock whose territory is his tractor. So, a campaign is mounted. We start feeding the chooks and ducks in the chook shed. This way, the peacocks have to go inside if they want a feed. They are initially suspicious, but it doesn't take too many days before the peacock is captured and placed with great indignity in a cage. He's then strapped on to the back of the ute and taken to his new home fifteen kilometres up the road. My uncle returns with a crate full of crazy roosters, all of whom he plans to fatten at the end of the chook shed, and one very beautiful, very demure peahen. He locks her in the bitch's box and I can tell that she thinks her world has ended.

She calls and the sound ripples like electricity. It's late in the day, the peacock is on his way past the haysheds to his roost in the gum tree. He stops as though he's been shot. She calls again. He stands uncertain, but when she calls again, he turns and runs towards the sound. That night he roosts on the bitch's box.

After a week we let out the peahen. She walks straight past the peacock as if he doesn't exist and heads to where she can see the hens and ducks feeding from a trough of grain. The peacock spreads his tail, raises it heavenward and declares his possession to an audience of roosters. My uncle and I exchange a grin. Sometimes it's too easy to make the living things around us happy.

∾

I'm inclined to draw a boundary between the domestic and the wild out here, as if the two exist in parallel. This is not entirely unwarranted – the wild have to live on their wits: they have no one to feed them or check their water; they are reliant on their connection to the world around them. The domesticated have their survival needs taken care of. But their two worlds do sometimes collide. This morning I noticed the ducks bunch together in alarm and make for the shelter of the stables. Then I saw the hens, who'd been fighting over the best scraps, stop and dart into the shelter of the chook house. Suddenly, the air was filled with wild bird calls. A parrot flew over me, screeching alarm, five galahs made for the shelter of a big gum outside my garden. Above me, two harrier falcons materialised from the direction of the creek. Like brown bombers, they floated high over the farmyard – a farmyard suddenly still, except for the peacocks, who refused to be alarmed. Then in came the fighter squadrons – traditional enemies who'd formed sudden alliances. The magpies were the first in pursuit, followed by the native mynahs. Flying in formation, the five of them swooped on the falcons. The magpies bombed from above, the mynahs attacked from below. They were supported by honeyeaters and butcher birds. Peewees called support from the shelter of the tree line. Before I'd even made it to the back door, the invaders were driven off and the all-clear had been sounded. The hens poked out their heads, the ducks tilted theirs skyward, and as the calls of the defenders quietened, the farmyard returned to its normal morning busyness.

The screen door slams behind me. I wonder, as I watch this scene, why do I insist on thinking of myself as disconnected from the physical world? I remember coming back 'inside' from the wilderness during our six months in Alaska. I felt as if the boundaries of my body had been shrunk by sleeping within four walls again, relying on artificial heat, being able to eat food immediately, without having to prepare it from scratch over a tiny camp stove. While living outside, I had expanded. Not literally – in fact physically I grew smaller as my body, hardened by the constant physical movement, became efficient and strong. But the edges of me had expanded so that I could immediately register a change in wind direction, or a drop in temperature, or the movement of time through the day. I don't have the same awareness out here as I developed in Alaska, but that boundary between the inside and outside is much closer.

Nevertheless, as my world expands, fear still licks at the edge. I've walked away from a man. I've carefully placed him where he can't be touched and closed off the space in my head that he was occupying. I won't look his way again. Each time my mind runs towards him, I block it as if my thoughts were a runaway herd of sheep. I stand in their track and, by waving and shouting, I turn them back. I stamp my feet until my head is grounded again in the here and now. I realise how much I've been changed by what's happened to me in the past five years. The evenings alone have reshaped me. Is it strange that when the tears have come on those nights on the couch and there has been no one there to distract me from them, I have become a little hardened? Is it any wonder that I would struggle so much to trust a man again?

My friends assure me I'll meet someone else. They're excited that I appear ready to re-engage with the world. This man I'm turning from doesn't pass muster for all sorts of reasons, and yet he's opened me up, he's caught my eye, he's gained a little of my trust, he's made me laugh and he's also made me vulnerable to a need I thought I'd covered so deeply it could only surface in the undercurrents of my dreams.

∞

In the last three days, I've seen three snakes. One in the chook shed hunting eggs, which my uncle killed while I screeched and danced at the end of the shed. One curled in the sun in the middle of the laneway as I walked down to bring in the horses, which flipped from the path and made my heart jolt while the blood sang in my ears. One by the silo, which dived down a hole slippery and quick as I ran for a piece of poly pipe. Everywhere I look, I see snakes. My favourite run is fast becoming too 'snakey' for me: I'll have to give it up until the days shorten and the earth cools.

I've got pieces of poly pipe stashed all around the house. Poly pipe is ubiquitous on any property and, although it has more banal uses for water, fuel and as a handy stick to move stock through the yards, its chief function in my eyes is as a perfect snake-killing implement. A lovely long bit means I don't have to be anywhere near the snake to break its back, and it has just the right mix of hardness and flexibility to make it a perfect weapon. If you saw all the poly pipe lying around the corners of the garden, you could be forgiven for thinking we were inundated with snakes. But actually I haven't seen that many – it's more that in these few days, as I've wrestled with this man, I feel as though they are always just ahead of me.

For I am wrestling with him. Despite my best intentions, the weight of his body butts against my solitude.

I hear the birds making a fuss outside the kitchen paddock. They screech and bomb and carry on as they do if a strange bird comes into the garden. I go outside and watch and realise they've found a goanna. Then I see it's another snake. I run for my poly pipe, angry at this intruder. I round the side of the house and slow down. The birds continue to track the snake's progress, and I raise my piece of pipe. But suddenly I can't kill it. It's not that I'm afraid, or not very. This one is reasonably small and heading away from me – an easy target – but for some reason I can't bring myself to break its back. I follow it down through the garden and feel dead inside, powerless and vulnerable. I scream at it and warn it not to come back and I turn and walk away, wondering if I've made a terrible mistake. That night I dream of snakes – great pits of them – but in my dream they all slide over me.

The next day the snake is back. I'm sorry, because I wanted to just let him be but now I will have to kill him. We've got about fifteen ducklings in the end of the chook shed and it is these little fellows, or more likely the mice that hang around to clean up the meal I scatter for the ducklings, that the snake has returned for. I'm pretty sure it's the same snake I saw yesterday. I watch the ducklings as it glides into their end of the chook shed. No doubt it is gauging whether they are too big for it to tackle. I'm sure they are, but I'm fascinated by their lack of fear. They watch the snake and move away from it as it slides towards them, but they don't take fright; almost nonchalantly, they carry on catching flies.

29

WE'RE GOING TO A WEDDING. It's so long since I've been to a wedding, it almost feels unnatural. Nobody gets married anymore and I can't say I blame them. But this wedding is special. I take the kids out of school. I've rented a huge house in the small coastal hamlet where the wedding is being held. Normally when we go to this place on the coast, we stay in our family beach house. But it will be occupied with wedding guests this weekend, so I've managed to rent a house in which we can sleep fourteen and we're close to my brother and his bride, in the thick of everything. Friends from South Australia, from the Snowy Mountains, from Sydney are all coming to stay. It will be a mix of generations. The youngest will be eighteen months and the oldest seventy-plus. I'm buzzing in anticipation of being in a house in a big group of people. I love the aloneness of my life up here, but I can't wait to sit in the midst of what will be a huge family gathering for a few days.

The kids and I pack the car the night before and early in the morning I hustle out the horses and tell them to enjoy their four days in the paddock. Duke droops as he watches me put out the rubbish, empty the chook bucket, water the pots, fill his water and feed container and sweep the concrete around the house. I've been up since before dawn – packing, putting new sheets on the beds for our return, going over the lists of what we need to take and what needs to be left here, folding laundry. Finally all is done and we get on the road. We shut the gate behind us and I laugh because I don't have any keys to lock the house and I wouldn't bother if I did. The sun peeps over the back of Malachi Hill and its warming rays hit the late frost.

I see the swoop of the plains with the Blue Mountains in the distance. Then steep hairpin bends that cut a way up into the mountains. The kids beg for the Bell's Line of Road rather than the main highway. It's narrow, with very few places to overtake trucks or other slow vehicles, but it always feels like an almost secret way to the city and when we're not in a hurry we stop and have a picnic and watch the light, or the mist, or whatever weather – and there's always weather – play itself out against the massive cliffs. The Blue Mountains, in contrast to the mountains in Alaska or Canada, are all about depth. They're buried mountains, so ancient that their mysteries reveal themselves in the deepest places, not the high ones.

But today we don't stop. I'm not in a mood for dawdling. We hit the mountains and I put my foot down and enjoy the sensation of knowing the road so well, of catching those who are sightseeing and passing them before they realise I'm behind them.

We drop down out of the mountains, spat out onto one of the new mega-roads around Sydney, cross the Hawkesbury and call out to the river that we'll see again soon as it finds its way to the sea. Then we crawl round the edge of Sydney till we hit the freeway and point our nose to the coast. We cross the Hawkesbury again and are transported into a world of Sydney sandstone, scraggly scrub and secret, watery places. The excitement mounts in the car. The kids are beside themselves with the thought of a new house to explore.

The house I've rented is a party house. We open the door and I'm immediately glad I've extended an invitation for all the wedding guests to come for a drink and dinner here. It's got a massive deck, an open kitchen and lots of room. I feel as though I could invite the world over and still have space to spare. I'm filled with confidence at having this place to entertain. The door stays open and before we've been there three hours, the house is filled with guests determined to leave behind their ordinary workday selves for the weekend.

I'm not alone in thinking this a special wedding. I think, too, it is something of a magic place, this spot on the coast. There is no supermarket, there are no apartments, no swanky shops; just a general store, a great café and the beauty. The evening rages on and, as more people arrive, the house seems to expand to hold them all. Eventually some sort of sanity prevails and people realise there is going to be a wedding tomorrow. Most leave to walk down or up the hill to their accommodation, until there are five or six left around the kitchen bench. In this hardy group are my brother's close friends, men I've known since they were boys, and who are now mostly married and either fathers, or on the way to being fathers. Responsible now, or apparently so, but this weekend they're determined to lay their mature selves to one side and see my brother out of his official bachelorhood with style.

The next morning I'm up early again. The sun rises over the ocean, and the mess of last night. It was worth it, but there's a lot of cleaning up to do. My head aches and I think I probably jumped out of the starting gate a little quickly, for we've still got a champagne brunch, a beach wedding and a rocking party before the day is out. The bottles clink against each other as I sling them in the bin. It's going to be a beautiful day and already people are out on their decks enjoying the morning over coffee and newspapers. There's a carnival atmosphere. Because it's early in the season, most of the holiday homes are empty except those rented by wedding guests, so it feels as if we have this place to ourselves. People call and wave to each other from deck to deck. We walk down the hill to the café for coffee. It's bliss, or close to it, to have a decent coffee within walking distance and I'm like a sponge soaking up the companionship and cosmopolitanism.

Many of the people coming to the wedding have been through two funerals with our family and I don't think I'm alone in feeling an unfamiliar sense of buoyancy at the prospect of today. But by the time we kick everyone off the deck to go and get changed into our wedding finery, I'm feeling nervous at what we are gathering to witness.

We walk down to the beach, where my brother and his new wife exchange vows. He sings a song to her so intimate it's as if we, the audience, do not exist. She reads him a poem. They are married in between the ocean and the land. I walk up the beach with my father to the surf club and we all eat and drink and dance and, if the absence of my husband and my mother scents the air, everyone still sees a good life for this couple and celebrates it.

At midnight I take two very tired children home to bed. Two doors up, in the house where we spent our childhood summers, a party explodes. A drumbeat hangs in the air like a question and I leave the kids and trot up the road. The house is packed, there's no room even to move, but people are dancing on the table, out on the deck, on the couch, pounding their bodies to the music. It's so much fun I can barely breathe and I feel as though I'm fifteen years old again.

The next day we have a long lunch with friends and in the evening slowly start to pack up. I'm glad for the length of the drive home. I need to sift through the emotions of the last few days. It's been a rollercoaster ride, but a mostly happy one. I've turned up to this event and been more certain of myself, more engaged, than I have been for years. The kids are starting to signal their increased independence. I missed my mother. I missed my husband, especially when there was so much love around, but perhaps what emerges through the layers is that although I missed my husband – his face, his spontaneity, his easy way with people – what I missed too was simply having someone with me to share this moment.

Reversing my journey, we cross the river, twice, then climb back into the mountains and at last feel the openness that greets us on the other side. The sky is quite simply different over here. It's bigger, you can expand into it and it encourages me to look into the distance rather than just in front of me. It settles me. As I drive into the blue, I realise I'm coming back here, coming back home. We drive up to the gate, where

Duke greets us. He escorts us back and forward from the car into the house. The evening light drops away and the scent of hay rises on the cooler air.

I stand and say with Sappho – I want.

30

I'M OFF TO SPEND THE EVENING UP IN THE STABLE plaiting Belle's mane for the one-day event we are going to tomorrow before dawn. Usually Lottie does it, but it takes her a long time, it's the end of term and she's tired. Lottie has also worked her, washed her, rugged her, fed her and packed the float with everything we'll need for the next two days. For, though it's a one-day event, this is a misnomer – they have so many kids participating that they have to run it over two days. I send Lottie down to the house to get dinner for herself and Charlie and, if I'm honest, quite happily embrace the solitude of being up in the stables with a moon rising, the chooks and ducks in bed and the dogs tied up (except for Duke, who is happily pottering around the edges). Belle is swathed in horse rugs, none of them fancy, but all of them piled on her with much attention.

I lead her out of her stall and tie her to the steel panel that divides one side of the old stable from the other. This shed shimmers in the night. Sometimes I'm jealous when I go and visit other people's set-ups and see their closed-in stables, with lights, hot and cold water and all manner of other luxuries. But then I have a night like tonight up in this old shed and I shrug my shoulders at such heretic desires. The old tin and timber building creaks in the wind, it hints at the secrets of the night, it harbours the light of the moon and the dark shadow of midnight. It's a cathedral space with its high ceilings and its wide open doors at each end. The two horses only live in one end of it – there is room here for at least eight horses. I always think buildings need to be used and I tell myself that this shed has been given a new lease of life with our two horses living every day in it.

When I was growing up, it was full of horses. Cosseted, highly strung racehorses, being spelled from their insane lives of running as fast as they could. Or young horses in the middle of being broken in to saddle and bridle. It was a bustling, busy, efficient place. Now it's very dusty, but I like to think our two ponies are keeping this big shed useful, maintaining a need for its sheltering roof and walls.

My uncle converted the shed when he first arrived here after marrying my aunt. He'd travelled the world with racehorses, flown valuable stallions from one hemisphere to the other. He used all that he'd learnt about horses in France, in England, Ireland and South Africa, to convert a hayshed into a stable that made horses happy.

Unlike most stables, which are closed off and very solitary in their use of space, this shed is communal. The horses are separated from each other by high mesh walls. They can see, smell, hear each other. They just can't kick or bite their neighbour. The outside walls have a window through which a horse can stick its head and gaze all day if it desires. A horse living in these stables can also look inward and see the entire shed. They can see exactly what their neighbour three stalls down is doing. So, because a horse is a herd animal and normally doesn't like spending time on his own, this is a comforting shed to live in. Because it's open the air circulates through it. It's dusty. But the horses don't get sick. It smells strongly of manure, but because the ducks snap the flies off the manure every morning, and because the chooks scratch through the wet spots and new manure from dawn till dusk, I never have to clean out a stall and the horses thrive. The flooring is earth, not brick or concrete, and our two happily lie down every night and have no bedsores or pressure points to show for it.

The moon rises. An owl beats softly through the air as he begins his hunting, the peacock calls a last challenge to the evening and then all around peace falls. I hum under my breath as the mare rests a hind leg and heaves a deep sigh. She knows what having her mane plaited means, she knows what the float outside her window means. I mutter at her, the plaiting needle firmly between my teeth. Her peace, her solid bulk centre me. As I plait, Will in the next stall munches his way through his evening ration of hay. He finishes far too quickly and I feel sorry for him as Belle will take the whole night to finish her ration and still leave some in the morning. Then I don't feel sorry for him because, despite always being placed in the barest paddock on the place, he is enormously fat.

The job is almost finished and I realise that the tension of a busy week, a busy term, has gone from my shoulders. The electric light above my head has attracted a thousand insects, and it also makes me feel that in this shed I'm in a house on top of a hill. Outside, the wind is whistling pretty fiercely but, though I can hear it working its way beneath the old timber and galvanised iron, we don't feel its breath on us here in the shed.

I pack up slowly. Put Belle back in her stall, fill up her hay racks. Typically she ignores the offering and stands with her head out of the window, her nose a trembling repository for all that is happening in the inky blackness of the farmyard. I say goodnight to them, turn off the light and walk down to the house, past the dogs, past the ducks who are enjoying an after-dark swim on their water trough, and down through the garden. Duke bounces ahead of me, excited by the thought of his daily ration of dry dog biscuits.

Tomorrow we leave early in the morning and I hope that Lottie hasn't forgotten anything too important. I take back to the house something of the peace the horse gave me as I stood beside her and plaited her mane.

31

Once, before we travelled to Alaska, before Lottie was born, before life showed itself to hold dark possibilities, we had a conversation. We were driving back to Sydney after visiting my parents in Melbourne. We'd been on the road for about six hours and had pulled in to a servo for fuel and dinner. It was a Sunday night and the servo was busy, full of people intent on getting somewhere else, lots of harassed mothers and little kids flying round, high on junk food and with energy to burn after being strapped into car seats for hours. We fuelled up and headed inside to order dinner. My husband was excited at the prospect of a big feed of chops, eggs, bacon and fried tomatoes. A horse truck had pulled in behind us and kids spilled out of the cabin. Our dinner arrived. The family from the horse truck trooped inside and sat down at the table next to us. There were four kids, and a mum and dad. The kids were filthy. They had jodhpurs on and once-white shirts and boots. Their faces were smeared with a healthy layer of dust. But they were noticeable not because of how dirty they were – which was quite unremarkable – but by how different they were to the other grubby, crabby kids scattered through the roadhouse. These kids radiated.

They'd come from a horse competition and were on their way home after camping for the weekend. The truck was just a flatbed with a cattle crate on the back. They didn't have fancy gear, but they had a horse each by the look of the truck. Their talk around the table was all about whose horse had gone well and whose had played up and where they would go next. My husband was transfixed. It was so far outside his coastal world, where kids talked of surf breaks and days at the beach.

When we were back on the road, our conversation circled around the horse-truck family. I told him about how much fun I'd had growing up riding, first on the farm and later at all the little events we used to do around the district. Being around horses had given me a great deal of independence; it had taught me about responsibility and self-sufficiency. We talked about having our own children and how we would love to give them the sort of childhood we'd just witnessed.

I've thought about that conversation many times since. I thought about it when I decided to buy the old red float I now pull all over the countryside. And when I spent the money and bought a decent four-wheel drive so I could tow it safely. I recalled it when I bought Lottie a new horse and Charlie started riding old Will, and every time I pack the float with horse gear, throw our swags in the car and head off with a few other families from nearby to one-day events or show-jumping days. And I think about it when we arrive at these places and are sitting round a fire after a long drive.

I think about it again tonight as I wander back to the house and pour myself a glass of wine. The kids are now lying in front of the fire watching a DVD. Charlie has filled the wood box, which is his special responsibility, and there is a peaceful feeling over my small family that I want to bask in. There have been so many times when his absence has smothered my evenings as if the hole he left in our family sucks all the oxygen out of the air and we must limp along living some sort of half-life without him.

I curl up on the couch and watch the fire. Charlie is asleep on the floor and I'm going to have to carry him to bed in a minute. He's getting so big that this is starting to be hard. But tonight, instead of it saddening me that I'm alone in gazing at his peaceful little boy face, alone to lift him to my shoulder, alone to feel his dead weight and the delicious thing little boys do when they're asleep of snuggling into the crook of your neck, I feel big enough to just enjoy him. I'm not looking over my shoulder to check whether my husband is watching. I'm not wishing his father was there to carry him to his bed and tuck him in. I can simply be his mother and hold him to me. And tomorrow I'll wake him and he'll slide out of bed eager for the day, pull on his boots, his jodhpurs, his enormous hat and be ready to go.

It's hard to put my finger on precisely what has changed me. Perhaps it's the ticking of time; perhaps it's the sweet breath of a horse; perhaps it's the waving tail of a corgi; or the sound of the cowbell on the door signalling that I'm not invisible – that I'm very much alive and apparently still attractive to a man who should know better. Probably it's all these things. I climb into bed and pick up a book, as through my window comes the smell of the earth cooling. I breathe it in and feel released.

The light pushes back the night as we load the ponies into the float and head out onto the road the next morning. It's a long trip with two horses and our old float, but we meet friends in the next town and swap the kids around so that I've got a car full of little boys, and the girls fill the other two cars. We arrive just after lunch and set up a camp.

The kids unload their horses and take them for a walk. Then I watch them carry heavy water buckets to the yards, cart the feed, rug their ponies and sit on their backs and talk to their friends. They set up their swags to sleep out under the stars. A game of footy is organised and kids from all over the western part of the state run under the light of the huge moon. They make new friends and play spotlight, and then talk into the night. The adults sit around the fire and swap stories. The talk is easy, a long way from the sort of conversations I would be having on Saturday night in the city at a book launch, but sitting round the fire under a huge night sky filled with stars, I don't wish I was anywhere else. The kids eventually come back to the fire and fill up on hot Milos. They go off to brush their teeth and check their horses and then come back to snuggle under my arms and say goodnight. Then dirty, and most definitely exhausted, they crawl into their swags.

In the morning, I wake and find them snuggled down deep under canvas. Their swags are wet with dew, but underneath they're all toasty and warm. The barbecue is sizzling with eggs and bacon as one of the dads cooks up a big breakfast. In their pyjamas and riding boots, the kids feed their horses. Then it's into clean jodhpurs, shirts, ties and boots, and the rest of the day passes in a blur of personal triumphs and small disappointments.

I'm always exhausted by the time we get home. And I'm always jealous of the other families who have dads to help them load and unload and drive to and from these places. But I'm also quietly proud of us for managing to be that family who arrives at the truck stop with a load of filthy, happy kids. My kids have gone to sleep with a heaven of stars as the last thing they see before they close their eyes. They know what an owl sounds like as it sweeps low over our campsite hunting for mice, and they know what it's like to be dirty and happy and tired and proud of yourself, all at the same time.

∽

Susan Songtag asks in her collection of essays *Regarding the Pain of Others* why we desire to be shocked, why we slow down on the freeway to look at the carnage of a life that could be ours, why we watch bombs falling on a city while we eat dinner. She argues that perhaps the only people with the right to look at suffering are those who could alleviate it or those who can learn from it. 'The rest of us are voyeurs, whether or not we mean to be.' Sontag is, of course, talking of images, paintings, photographs, but the role she attributes to the audience is true enough of the reader as of the viewer. It is also true of the memorialiser.

At times, I feel like a voyeur in my own life. What right do I have to portray these events, to try to place them in a frame I might understand? I return to the question asked by Anne Carson of Euripides' tragedies: why is tragedy so important as an art form? Her answer brings me up against my own terrible truth. Tragedy is important because it enables us to imagine our own reactions in a dark well of horror. It lets us watch others suffer. By watching, we are prepared. By watching, we place a frame around our world and pace its boundaries. We guard against unknown horrors that call to us from beyond our walls. I watch so I might know, and write so I might be understood. But my terrible truth is that no matter how carefully I place that frame, no matter how deeply I dive under the sea, I will never really understand why.

∾

It's raining. It's too late. The crops have failed, the paddocks are bare, the growing season over. Ahead of us stretches a summer of constant feeding, hungry animals and little promise of respite from this routine for months. Yesterday we had another dust storm. The house is coated in the dirt from a neighbour's paddock. My uncle pulls his hat over his eyes and mumbles about environmental vandalism. Dust moves in great brown sheets across the landscape. The world is made dark by it. Today the temperature has plummeted and the radio is filled with sheep grazier warnings, and the rain has arrived.

Lottie bakes a spice cake, which fills the kitchen with the

comforting smell of nutmeg and cinnamon. I should feel a sense of relief as the rain tattoos a blessing on my roof. But I don't. It will be hot again tomorrow, the sheep will still need to be fed and the grass won't have grown. If there is any redemption in this cycle of drought and plenty, it's that eventually the land will recover. I can't see it, but I know that where there is bare, hard earth, grass will grow. I know that when the rain comes, the memory of this terrible drought, the tension tied up in waiting for rain, will be remembered only as a shudder in a nightmare.

Kayaking in Alaska, we made our camp on the beach at the end of each day's paddle. It was a different beach every night, and in the evening around a smouldering fire we studied the chart and tried to guess a good beach on which to spend the next night. Most often we got it right and there was enough space between the ocean and the forest to pitch our tents and drag the kayaks above the high-water mark. But there were times when we had to land suddenly because of the weather conditions or because of exhaustion. Or sometimes the beach we had landed on looked bigger on the chart than it was in reality. On those nights, we measured the high-water mark, studied the tide table and hoped like hell we wouldn't get an onshore wind that would sweep the tide right into our tents.

I had never lived that close to the sea before. If we were not paddling across its surface, we were squatting beside its lapping edge scrubbing our pots and pans with gravel from the beach, the water cold, the salt stiff on our skin. At night I would crawl into my sleeping bag and my hands would tingle painfully, reverberating with the rhythm of paddling, the pull of the water against my paddle, the heavy slap of wind chop on the hull of the kayak. I would fall into a deep, exhausted sleep. As I slept, the sea would rise and pull me into its depths.

I can feel the tide tugging and, though I know I'm asleep, the physical world is so close to me that I'm awake to its movements. Though I am afraid of the ocean, I have to accept its overwhelming presence if I am to sleep. If I don't sleep, I won't be able to paddle tomorrow; if I don't sleep, I won't survive. I learn the trick of sleep. I pretend I'm a dog and curl myself around rocks, ignore discomfort and give in to exhaustion. I lie in my tent and allow the ocean to sweep me away.

Tonight, 350 kilometres away from the coast, in a landscape as empty of water as a desert, I dream that the house is like a shore and the land around me is the ocean. I lie in bed and the wind pours over me like the tide. Instead of salt, it carries the top soil from the earth. At the beginning of the drought, I fought this tide of dust, which finds its way into the deepest cupboard. To lose the fight with it is inevitable, yet fight it I do, for sometimes when I wander through the house I see that everything has been leached of colour. I look out onto only brown: it's in my hair, on my clothes, the furniture, on my books, the table, benches, floor – everything is gritty with the layer of earth it carries. As I sleep it covers me, so when I wake there's grit in my eyes and teeth. I touch my finger to my tongue and taste not grit but cinnamon.

∽

I have one more thing to do. I have to scatter his ashes. He shouldn't be in a box. But it is so complicated. His beautiful child doesn't want to let go of him. She was five when he died. Aged six, she resolutely wouldn't let go. At seven she was forced to say goodbye to her grandmother, her second self. Then she was eight and we were just concentrating on breathing, on getting through the day without someone dying.

Now she is nine and suddenly she is ready. Her decision takes me by surprise. I'd fallen into the habit of expecting her resistance. But this time when I suggest we spread his ashes, she peacefully agrees. Charlie doesn't understand, but I want him to have the memory of us doing this together, even if I have to recreate it for him over and over again. We go back to the sea, just her and me and my other child who is of him but not him. We take him to the place he loved. We open the box and they pick up pieces of him and throw him into the air.

He mixes with salt and wind. He falls on rock and heath. He falls into beauty as the children scatter him like chicken feed. They laugh and chase each other on the high headland in the screaming wind. I say goodbye. At last, I say goodbye.

Epilogue

It's 3 am on Christmas morning, the kids are asleep and I've been wrapping their presents and playing Santa. Our house looks like it's Christmas. The tree is dripping in lights. My mother's favourite nativity scene is set up on the coffee table in front of the fireplace. The dining-room table has a golden tree as its centrepiece and tinsel is festooned around the windows and mantelpiece.

Earlier, I sat at my desk while the kids decorated the tree and the house. I could hear them exclaiming over each decoration they pulled from the box. Lottie remembers where every bauble has come from, and she gave Charlie a small history lesson while they placed them carefully on the tree. Most of the decorations are my grandmother's and most of them were made here in her sewing room, which is now Charlie's room. Lottie, who was lucky enough to have known my grandmother, tells Charlie stories of her cleverness with a needle and thread, and of the things she used to cook for

Christmas. Lottie's stories, though not necessarily accurate, seem to conjure my grandmother from the air around her. The two of them were so serious in their decorating that I didn't want to cut into their space. Lottie's superior knowledge, her age, her firsthand experience of my grandmother and Charlie's father gave her stories an authority Charlie couldn't challenge. But she didn't flaunt it; rather it was like a ceremony, a handing-on of knowledge. I listened, afraid to break the spell.

This year we have decided to stay home for Christmas. The kids really want to be here. They want to wake in their own beds and I consider this an achievement of sorts. My work has claimed me in the days leading up to Christmas. But this doesn't seem to worry the kids. They just get on with it. All I've had to do is dredge up a Christmas tree, find the decorations and leave them to it. My deadline means that I've put off buying presents until the very last minute. This afternoon I was in town armed with warnings of the dreadful crowds and chaos of Christmas Eve. But having done a Christmas Eve shop in Melbourne, Sydney and London, it seemed positively congenial here. There were lots of farmers in shorts and boots discussing perfumes, lingerie and jewellery. The town was buzzing, and, it is true, I did have to wait about three minutes for a parking space, and there was a line at the Myer check-out, but it was a small and friendly line, we all had a chat and everyone was very supportive of the last-minute nature of our mission.

But, more than Christmas and presents, and the busyness of the main street, what everyone really wants to talk about is rain. The bureau is forecasting rain. Big rain. Our well, which has never run dry in over seventy years, did so this year and my uncle had to drill for more water. This is happening everywhere. One day of rain is no longer enough. We need weeks of it. The ground water has most dramatically dropped. Tanks are empty, dams are either muddy puddles or dried-up bogs. Perennially wet creeks have been dry for months. The landscape is pinched. But if rain comes now, the dams might fill, the lucerne flats will be revived, the feed might grow and last a couple more months. Rain now will bring hope. And it's starved hope that sits under the talk.

I get home from town. We go up to my aunt and uncle's house for a Christmas Eve dinner. As we walk home across the flat, the stars are spread like a benediction above us. It's hot and not that humid. I put the kids to bed after setting out a little bit of dinner for Santa and his reindeer. Then I do some work and suddenly it's late and I haven't wrapped any presents. I know I've been putting it off. But once I start it's not hard. I stuff the stockings, take a couple of bites out of the carrot left out for the reindeer and crawl under the covers.

Tomorrow is Christmas. The kids will wake excited. All will be good. The house is ready to host my aunt, uncle and cousins in the morning for coffee and unwrapping presents. But sleep won't come. It's quiet and it's lonely.

I lie still.

I lie here.

The rain starts to fall.

Softly, then with a drumming beat. The smell of the earth fills my room again. Outside, the hard ground breathes and receives the rain as if it were always going to come. Tomorrow, I think, because of the rain, tomorrow will be different.